Into the Arms of Jesus

By:

Jetta Nastally

Into the Arms of Jesus

By

Jetta Nastally

Published By:

ABM Publications
A division of HSBN Publishing
PO Box 6811, Orange, CA 92863

ISBN: 978-1-931820-87-5

DEDICATION

A big thanks to all my lovely family and friends who stood by me when all looked hopeless concerning my recovery. You all prayed and believed God for a miracle and indeed He answered your prayers. *Without your intervention, this book would never have been written.*

I dedicate this book to all of you. I honor my son, Kevin, and his lovely wife Hetty, as well as my sister, Sandy, for standing and believing God for total restoration of my mental health and recovery. Without their faith, this book would not have been possible.

I honor my spiritual mother, Eugenia Ranney, who came to my rescue during my recovery and brought back the history of who I was before going under witchcraft. Without her love, prayers, and counsel, I would have never known my earthly destiny in Christ.

I honor my nephew, Howard Powell, and his lovely wife, Beverley. They gave me the privilege of marrying them on St. Patrick's Day, March 17, 2018. I was able to see God's anointing, through the Holy Spirit, flow over the people in attendance and change their hearts. God's truth, when anointed, opens the hearts of the lost.

I honor my adopted family the Lizarragas; Benny and Monette, Bailey and Brenda, and little Eliza and Isabel, as well as Noah and Tatum. I also honor Jason, another adopted member of this family. Together, we experienced the miracles that God performed through us, by walking in His faith, confessing His Word, and releasing His angels to overthrow the enemy's plans.

I would like to honor also all those dear saints of God in Eastgate Ministries and in World for Jesus Ministries that warred over my soul with heavy intercession. All of your prayers are greatly appreciated.

I love you all,

- *May the Lord bless and keep you all*
- *May He make His face to shine upon you*
- *May He be gracious unto you.*
- *May the Lord lift up His countenance upon you and give you peace through Jesus Christ our Lord and Savior.*

(Taken and adapted from the Aaronic blessing in Numbers 6:24-26)

ACKNOWLEDGEMENTS:

Honor and thanks are due to:

1. The Holy Spirit – for pouring out His anointing upon this book.

2. To my son Kevin for his diligence in extending many hours towards the editing of this book. Kevin carved out time in his busy work schedule to help mom make the publication of this book possible. I'm eternally grateful.

3. To my dear friend Irina Sledge who through much warfare and effort, sacrificed her time in the editing of this book. I greatly appreciate all that she has done. God shall surely honor her for all her efforts.

4. I give honor to Charity Bradshaw who helped pull this book out of me through her counsel and professional expertise. Without this first step, this book would never have been written.

JETTA NASTALLY

TABLE OF CONTENTS

QUICKLY GLEAN THROUGH THE CONTENTS OF THIS BOOK

We often purchase books only to read a few chapters.

Italics
By reading through the italics, you can quickly glean the contents of this book.

By looking at the overall emphasis of a book you can glean its contents rather than focusing on the details within the book. I have highlighted the important details to condense it into a few hours of reading. You then can revisit the sections that are of particular interest to you.

It is my hope that you will be drawn to read the entire book as it is a unique story of how Satan tries to steal one's destiny by placing roadblocks (blockages) in their path. This story entails a life placed under the spirit of witchcraft.

Important sections of this book that you might want to revisit are:

- *The warfare section, which includes tools on how to use God's Word to protect yourself from Satan's deceptions and lies.*
- *The GOD SPEAKS section that reflects the heart of the Father toward His children.*

This book teaches you how to overcome evil spirits and demonic strongholds.

WORD DEFINITIONS

Atmosphere
This is a gaseous envelope that surrounds the Earth. It contains the firmament of God. The first heaven includes the sky, the sun, the moon, and the Earth. In fact, everything physical is in this firmament. The second heaven is Satan's demonic realm. The third heaven is where God dwells. We fight warfare against demonic forces from this realm. We are in Christ Jesus in heavenly places taking our authority over the enemy in this realm.

Blood of the Lamb
This is the blood of Jesus Christ, the spotless Lamb of God, that has redeemed us back to Father God through the Cross of Calvary. His blood is holy and precious. To obtain the free gift of salvation (the gateway back to God), you must first receive Jesus Christ as your Lord and Savior.

Body
This refers to your physical human body.

Cloud of Witnesses
These are special saints of God who loved and followed God's commandments on Earth to the best of their abilities. Many suffered persecution, rejection, and physical setbacks but they never denied Christ. Many were martyred. These saints have been taken into the Cloud of Witnesses and are now warring in heaven for the salvation of those on Earth to be accomplished for God's glory.

Corporate Anointing
When a body of people come together with the same intent and become unified in oneness of purpose and heart, they establish a corporate anointing that brings forth spiritual

power. This applies to evil as well as good. When God's people are unified, they can pull down the strongholds of the enemy.

Curses
Curses are listed in Deuteronomy chapter 28 (starting at verse 15) of God's Holy Bible - His Word. Curses consist of diseases, infirmities, illnesses, financial lack, and any other form of loss. Anything that is not prosperous, good, righteous and loving is not of God. (God's blessings are listed in the first part of Deuteronomy chapter 28 and they are also mentioned throughout scripture.)

Glory
The glory of God is the manifested presence, power, and goodness of God that can be felt and sometimes seen. It is the complete person of God (Father, Son, and Holy Spirit), and is also the place of His heavenly abode. Where He is, Heaven is. The glory is the goodness, the fullness, the splendor, and the awareness of His manifested presence.

Godhead
This refers to the Father, the Son, and the Holy Spirit. They work together as one with different assignments.

Holy Spirit
This is the third person of the Godhead. He is referred to as the Comforter who resides in our vessel after we have received Jesus Christ as our Savior. He is our mentor. He guides and leads us into all truths. He receives His direction from the Father, and He releases that information into our spirit. He speaks to us in many ways. The language of the Holy Spirit must be learned. He is a great teacher. His instructions always line up with God's Word.

Imagination

Mental images are produced by the action of imagination. This is when you take your imagination into the spiritual realm to see pictures. These pictures can come from Satan as well as God. However, God's pictures are based on truth and love and Satan's pictures are based on evil, hate, and deception. When God's people are given visions in the spirit realm, they appear in their mind's eye in a pictorial form.

Impurities and/or dross

Impurities are regarded as worthless; rubbish. They are formed within the soul when it is exposed to sin and hurtful circumstances. These are removed by the blood of Jesus. We then must walk in obedience to God's commandments which are found in His Holy Bible.

Praise

The act of expressing approval, thanksgiving, adoration, and/or admiration towards God. Often this is expressed through music and song by worshipping God using scriptural content from His Word. Praise is acknowledging God for what He has done, for what He is doing, and for what He will do.

Realm

The region, sphere, or domain within which anything occurs, prevails, or dominates. There is the Earth realm and the spirit realm. There are three specific spiritual realms: faith, anointing, and glory. Each realm contains a dominant theme and specific protocol for access. When speaking of the glory realm, this is the domain or kingdom of God that contains the fullness of God and all heavenly realities.

Rhema Word

When this Word comes to a person, it gives divine direction and revelation. It is a personal revelation from God, to you, regarding something you have been seeking and asking Him about. It always agrees with the written Word of God, the logos. When it is spoken, it is alive and it brings forth the supernatural miracles of God.

Shekinah Glory

This is the divine manifested presence of God. It is tangible and can be felt.

Shod

This means permeated or to completely cover the surface of an item. In the scripture referenced in this book, from Ephesians chapter six, it is our feet, covered in God's peace.

Smote

This word means to deliver a powerful and sudden blow; to inflict a crushing defeat to the opposing force.

Spirit

Your spirit person is eternal, it is the real you. If your spirit left your body, you would die. Your spirit knows more than your natural mind. Your spirit is the inside person of your heart, and when you get saved, it is the part of you that is born again and filled with God's Spirit. You contact and connect with God through your spirit.

Spirit of Truth

The Spirit of truth is the Holy Spirit within you.

Soul

As a human being, you are made up of three parts. You are a spirit, you have a soul, and you live in a physical body on this Earth. Your soul is your mind (intellect and natural reasoning), your will, and your emotions/feelings.

Strongholds

A stronghold is a fortress; a defensive structure; a high and inaccessible place. In scripture, there are good and bad strongholds. God is referred to as a stronghold in Psalm18. The strongholds, as used in this book, refer to the negative type, which are blockages in the spirit realm contrary to God's Word that need to be removed or taken down by prayer and intercession.

Theos and/or Trinity

In the context of this writing, Theos and Trinity refer to the Godhead, (the Father, the Son, and the Holy Spirit) that dwell within your inner person.

Worship

It is the reverent honor and homage we pay to God. Often worship comes through dancing and bowing before God in reverence. It is thanking God for His mercies and His grace that He extends to us each day.

Yoke

A yoke is a wooden beam normally used between a pair of oxen to enable them to pull together on a load when working in pairs. A yoke then can be a bondage that is around your neck that moves you in a direction that is unpleasing to your flesh. When removed, you are freed from this restriction.

Bible Translation Versions:

AMPC (American Amplified Bible, Classic Edition)

KJV (King James Version)

LB (The Living Bible, Tyndale)

MSG (The Message)

NIV (New International Version)

NKJV (New King James Version)

TPT (The Passion Translation)

JETTA NASTALLY

INTRODUCTION
(Below are *excerpts* taken from various chapters in this book)

God has already placed in your heart your purpose. You need only to follow the language of your heart - it will lead you to your destiny.

God's timing is perfect. He is not too late, and He is not too early. Although you might feel totally overwhelmed, totally defeated, and totally useless given your circumstances - *God is bigger than your circumstances.* He has set a fire under you and that fire is burning the impurities out of your life. He will light your fire with His glory if you will trust Him and walk according to His Word - walking according to His Spirit within you, trusting Him with all your heart.

Do not despair. A miraculous movement of God is coming for the redeemed. His glory cloud will overshadow the darkness that is all about us, and a great breakthrough will manifest for the saints of God. God just wants to encourage you to stay faithful to His Word to the best of your ability. He wants you to learn to speak words of life which bring forth God's blessings. Just praise Him, love Him, and thank Him. Even if you do not feel you have anything to thank God for, you do. The enemy has just clouded your vision. Go for a walk in the park, smell the roses, and look at the beautiful trees and flowers. They are all praising God. How much more should we, who are created in His image, praise Him too!

God not only loves His children; He identifies with them. Jesus came to Earth and experienced and overcame great trials, tribulations and rejection from the rulers and leaders of that time. Jesus was immaculately conceived by the Holy Spirit. Therefore, when He died on the Cross of Calvary, His blood was pure. His blood was not tainted with the sin of Adam who disobeyed God in the Garden of Eden and lost his spiritual covering of God's glory. Adam sold mankind out to become slaves to Satan. Man's new god then became Satan. Ever since the Garden of Eden, Satan has deceived man to believe his lies.

*People have been deceived throughout the centuries by Satan who was an anointed cherub in heaven (*Ezekiel 28:14*).* His ministry in heaven was music. Pride rose up in him and he wanted to be greater than God, so God kicked Satan out of heaven and placed him on Earth. Satan had so much influence that he was able to coerce a third of all the angels in heaven to follow him. They left their home in the heavenly paradise to become slaves to a cruel devil. They were all deceived. And that is exactly what Satan tries to do with all human beings. He deceives them to believe his lies. He creates hatred; whereas in God there is total love for God is love. Satan has blinded the eyes of people on Earth who do not know Jesus, so that they think evil is good and good is evil. They have been deceived by the enemy to reject truth.

History has a way of repeating itself. When people disregard the rules of life that God outlined for us to live by in the Holy Bible; when they write their own ticket, eventually, they fall into deep sin and mankind again repeats history.

You were created for a purpose. God placed you on Earth at this specific time in history. You have an appointed destiny for God on Earth. God sent His Son Jesus to die on the Cross of Calvary to set you free from the clutches of Satan.

C.I. Scofield, a Greek and Hebrew scholar, states that "Salvation" as referred to in Romans 1:16 means the following:

- Deliverance
- Safety
- Preservation
- Healing
- Soundness (health).

Therefore, salvation in Jesus Christ brings all the above blessings to you.

May God bless you all with the revelation of truth of who you are in Christ Jesus and who He is in you. You carry within you the very same power that Jesus carried when He walked this Earth. He did only what the Father told Him to do. When Jesus ascended into heaven, he sent his Holy Spirit, the Comforter, into the hearts of all believers. Jesus sits at the right hand of the Father making intercession for you and me. He sent His Holy Spirit into our hearts to be our mentor. The Holy Spirit speaks to us of what He hears from Father God. The Holy Spirit is the person who brings the Glory Cloud and brings the anointing that breaks the strongholds in our lives.

You can defeat the enemy every time when you know your purpose and destiny in God. You were placed on this Earth to accomplish a mission for God. Way down inside you, God has placed within you your purpose and your calling. You just need to seek Him for it. When you find this purpose and walk in God's faith, in all humility and servanthood, walking in the truth of His Word and His commandments, the enemy cannot touch you. However, your words must be words of life and not death. That includes: your spoken words, your imagination, your feelings and your emotions - all must be submitted to God.

Watch the words of your mouth. They create. What you speak and what you imagine are creative forces. They create life or death. Therefore, guard your words. As you were created in God's image, you have that power to create your world. When you control your tongue and your imagination, you control your life and your destiny. For what you speak is what you create.

You must have a vision in front of you of where you are going with the Lord. You must find out what your Earthly destiny is for Him. And when you obtain this information and walk in the light of His Word toward that destiny, the devil is no match for you, for greater is He that is within you, than he that is within the world.

You are a blessing. You all are His chosen vessels. Release yourselves into your destiny and go forward to conquer the land for Jesus Christ who died to set the captives free.

When Jesus arose from the cross, He delivered all mankind from the death of eternal hell - all those who embrace Him as their Lord and Savior. This story will show you how to walk with God. It will give you detailed understanding of the fall of man, and it will give you the weapons to defend yourself against the ploys of the enemy.

God has stirred my heart to share my testimony so that: revival and reformation, hope and deliverance will come into your hearts and souls, and you will be lifted to see truth and fulfill your destiny on Earth.

This is a story of how I came out from underneath the spirit of witchcraft. It is a testimony of what happens to a person when they have been placed under demonic forces. It is a testimony of how God delivered me out from underneath that spirit, hid me away for two years and taught me the language of the Holy Spirit. He taught me how to walk in the Spirit of Love, how to listen to the Holy Spirit within my person, and how to activate His directives immediately without procrastination.

My first outreach is this book. God wants this book published to show people that there is always hope in Him no matter what circumstances you are in or have been through. God can lift you up above all those clouds of darkness, for Jesus paid the price for you with His precious blood on Calvary.

This book is a supernatural story of how I came out from underneath the clutches of evil. *The open door to freedom and liberty come only through Jesus. You are His gates of hope for all to walk into their destiny.* God wants to use you to set people free. For as long as I can remember I have had one desire in my heart, to see all people set free from hopelessness and despair.

This is a story of how God developed His spiritual gifts within me to be used as an intercessor to help set people free. This is a story of how I learned to walk in the Spirit of Truth and to overcome the spirit of darkness through accepting Jesus Christ as my Lord and Savior.

What makes this book different is that it provides a living example of how witchcraft steals your identity, erasing your memory of who you are in Christ Jesus.

Through marriage, and submitting myself under my husband's authority, I lost all the spiritual gifts the Lord had given me. Yes, I lost my identity of who I was in Christ. My husband's father and ex-wife both practiced witchcraft. Therefore, my husband was bound by this spirit and was never able to come out from underneath it. This story tells you how God supernaturally delivered me from that spirit of witchcraft.

If God can do it for me, He can do it for you. There is nothing God cannot do. He never leaves you, nor forsakes you after you become His child. However, placing your soul under your spirit is a process which does not happen overnight. It takes trials and tribulations to bring your soul under your spirit. (Remember your soul encompasses your mind, your emotions, and your will). Yes, there are trials, but if you walk in faith obeying His commandments; to the best of your ability, He will grant you your heart's desire. God will resurrect the dream that He originally placed in your heart. He will bring it to pass in a way you never imagined.

God is a supernatural God and His word is truth. According to Isaiah 55:11, His Word goes out and never returns void.

I wrote this book because your success is my success. God is a supernatural God and all things are possible with Him. You have a destiny for God. You have a purpose.

It is my prayer that the anointing that is on this book will set you free so that you too can complete your God-given destiny on Earth.

CHAPTER 1
COVENANT WITH GOD
(Note: This is a dialog of Jetta speaking to God, and God speaking back to Jetta.)

Jetta Speaking
I cried out to God: "Whatever it takes to get souls into the kingdom of heaven, I give you permission to put me through that fire. I release my life into your hands."
I asked God, "When did I make this covenant with you? How old was I?" *God then proceeded to go through many of the events from my childhood that revealed strongholds in my life that needed to be broken.* Below is a list of God's answers to my question.

God Speaking
Remember the day you threatened your mother that you would kill yourself if she did not give you your way? Your mother did not relent to your rebellion. So, you tested her. You went outside and tried to do something destructive to yourself to get your way. However, your mother was not moved by your foolishness and finally you submitted to her authority.

Then there was the time you tried to run away from home with your next-door neighbor Judy. You both packed up a little bag with some supplies and headed off. You discovered that the world outside was not so friendly. At dark, you decided that home was not such a bad place after all. You remembered your phone number, and someone was able to contact your parents to come and pick you up.

Remember the time when your mother gave you the responsibility of feeding and watering the canary birds that were given to you? Because the bird cage was located far

23

from your house, *you did not feed nor water these birds and they all died. Your mother did not pick up your responsibility.* She allowed you to see that the lack of action on your part caused the death of all those canaries. You were sorrowful, but that did not bring those birds back to life. You learned the lesson of taking responsibility the hard way.

How about the time you were working at San Diego State University? As you sat at your desk, you were totally distraught and hopelessly depressed. I spoke to you to look at the beauty all around you - the sky, the flowers, the animals. But you could not visualize any of this beauty that was surrounding you. *You were at a point of wanting to die thinking there was nothing to live for. You had no self-esteem; you considered yourself worthless. You could not visualize yourself as a person of worth.* You could not visualize that I loved you so much that I sent My Son Jesus Christ to die for your sins so that you could be free from guilt and sin. I did this so that everyone could become My family.

How about the time when you and your family were the first vehicle to drive past a freeway accident? As a young child, not even in your teens, you looked at all the body parts that were lying on the freeway. *People were beheaded, arms and legs were separated from their bodies, cars were totaled, and the people were all dead. This made a grave impression upon your young life.* You knew of Jesus, but you did not know him intimately. Even though you had no relationship with the Holy Spirit, I had placed within your heart a special love for all people.

Throughout all your childhood, you had a heart to see people happy. Your family was very dysfunctional, and you thought you could save them all from their pain by being an enabler. So that is what you became. Your father and mother fought over money constantly. Although your mother loved you, she also suffered from lack of self-esteem. Before your mother's death, you and your sister claimed her salvation standing on **Acts 16:31** (KJV)

"Believe on the Lord Jesus Christ, and thou shalt be saved, and thy house." **Acts 16:31** (KJV),

When your mother passed into heaven, I gave you a vision of the angels taking her into heaven. She was running through a meadow of beautiful flowers and as she ran, nothing beneath her feet was crushed.

How about the time I sent you to Bill Hammond's International Ministries in Florida? There I spoke to you in connection with your soon to be husband, James Nastally. You listened intently. But what you forgot was that through the multitude of counselors, there is safety. You did not allow anyone to counsel you. You simply plunged into this marriage headfirst. Ouch. *You took the hard route, rather than the easy route to obtain that promise which I had written in your heart. Many years of pain followed you. When you submitted yourself under James' authority, you lost your identity in who you were in Christ as James was under the spirit of witchcraft from his family lineage.*

"Plans fail for lack of counsel, but with many advisers they succeed."[1] (NIV)

All these tests worked together in your life for the glory of the kingdom of God. Now that you have overcome your trials and tribulations and have been set free, you can share your testimony with others, so that they also can be

set free. There is such freedom in Christ when you surrender all.

Jetta Speaking:
God heard that prayer and held me accountable to it. It was a covenant prayer.
All things we go through can be used to shape us into the vessel of glory that He has ordained us to be. Yes, God does hear our prayers, everything we go through is used to transform us into His image.

> "And we know that in all things God works for the good of those who love him, who have been called according to His purpose." [2] (NIV)

God told me that my story must be told to others as few are able to go through the kind of fire I went through and come out from under the hand of witchcraft. He said that because of my love for Him, I died to all my dreams. I surrendered all to my husband, placing myself under his authority, and loved him to the best of my ability.

Because of my background of being an enabler, I hated fighting, so I surrendered to James and gave him everything that made him happy. And yes, he was happy. I was the only person in his life that stood by him. Because of the lies told to his children, James lost contact with his two children. They believed the lies spoken to them about their father. Therefore, there was no contact between James and his children for over 20 years. Neither James nor I even knew the names of James' grandchildren; and he had many.

However, James was God's faithful son. He loved God with all his heart. He just did not know how to use the Word of God for himself. He had given up on ever being able to be healed physically on Earth. He had many physical issues in his body, but he endured, and he kept reading God's Word. He read it repeatedly - the Old Testament at least 300 times and the New Testament more than 1,000 times. Because he had so much pain in his body, his favorite place to read God's Word was in the bathtub. He endured pain beyond what one can imagine. And *when God had accomplished all the work in me that needed to be done here on Earth through James, He received James into heaven and indeed he was taken into the Cloud of Witnesses. James and I are still partners. I am the feet (upon this Earth), and James is whole and healed in heaven, fighting warfare in the Cloud of Witnesses for God's people and for me.*

Satan tried to take James and I out before our time. *Since my last near-death experience,* through the prayers of my sister, son, and many saints of God, I have come forth out of my wilderness into the arms of Jesus. *I had been given prophetic words that all that I lost would be restored over and above my losses. (Note: I was scammed out of all my retirement monies.) I knew that the only way for this to occur was to speak life, the Word of God, and let no negative confession come from my lips.*

> "For the law of the Spirit of life in Christ Jesus hath made me free from the law of sin and death."[3] (KJV)

I surrendered all unto the Lord. He hid me away for two years teaching me the language of the Holy Spirit. I was trained to listen to His voice and obey.

> "Your kingdom come, your will be done, on Earth as it is in heaven."[4] (NIV)

With God there is always grace when your heart is purposed towards the promise that He has placed deep within your being. There is a knowing inside you, a promise that God has placed there, and it truly is the cry of your heart. My cry was salvation of souls; keeping them from eternal damnation and hell. Heaven is real and so is hell.

God had a plan, and when my husband passed into heaven, God's voice quickly came back to me and He directed my steps. I made out a will and granted power of attorney and medical authorization over my health to my son and sister. Had I not done this, when the devil tried to take me out the fourth time, I would have lost everything. So, you see God does have a plan and His plan is greater than anything the devil could ever throw at us.

> "For in Him all things were created, things in heaven and on Earth, visible and invisible, whether thrones or powers or rulers or authorities; all things have been created through Him and for Him."[5] (KJV)
> "Yet in all these things we are more than conquerors through Him who loved us."[6] (NKJV)
> Jesus replied, "What is impossible with man is possible with God."[7] (NIV)

*The key to it all is God's faith. When He imparts that into your being, and when He shows you what you were created to do for His Kingdom, then by His grace you can persevere through all trials and emerge victorious. However, you must see yourself in the light of God's Word. You must know that the Godhead; the Father, the Son, and the Holy Spirit, reside in your vessel and that you are more than a conqueror through Christ who loves you. According to [**Galatians 3:13** (KJV)], "Christ hath redeemed you* *from the curse of the law, being made a curse for you: for it is written, Cursed is everyone that hangeth on a tree".*

*Curses are written in Deuteronomy 28, starting from verse 15. They consist of diseases, infirmities, illnesses, and financial lack. Anything that is not prosperous, good, righteous and loving is **not** of God.*

When you finally come to the end of running your own life, and turn your life over to God, that is when it all changes for you. You then become illuminated with God's love. His Shekinah Glory shines forth from your vessel. You must realize that you are the temple of God and that within you is all that God is. You are His servants here to speak forth His Words on this Earth and bring them into manifestation just as Jesus did. Jesus did only what the Father told Him to do. He spoke only what the Father told Him to speak. In order to do this, you must speak the Word and cast down wrong thoughts, feelings and imaginations.

> "Casting down imaginations, and every high thing that exalteth itself against the knowledge of God, and bringing into captivity every thought to the obedience of Christ"[8] (KJV)

And after you do this, the life you live, you live for the Son of God who loves you and gave His life for you.

> "I have been crucified with Christ and I no longer live, but Christ lives in me, the life I now live in the body, I live by faith in the Son of God, who loved me and gave Himself for me."[9] (NIV)

In Julie Meyers' book *Singing the Scriptures*, it shows us that David sang his way to victory. He sang the Word to God and therefore in every situation he came out victorious. That's not to say he didn't have his trials, but he never gave up hope that God would come through for him.

> *In Julie's book she states that singing the scriptures brings one hundred percent victory over your life's situation because God must honor His Word.[10]*
> *"So is My Word that goes out from My mouth: It will not return to Me empty but will accomplish what I desire and achieve the purpose for which I sent it."[11]* (NIV)

End Notes:
1. Proverbs 15:22 NIV
2. Romans 8:28 NIV
3. Romans 8:2 KJV
4. Matthew 6:10 NIV
5. Colossians 1:16 KJV
6. Romans 8:37 NKJV
7. Luke 18:27 NIV
8. 2 Corinthians 10:5 KJV
9. Galatians 2:20 NIV
10. Meyers, Julie, *Singing the Scriptures*, Chosen Books, 2018
11. Isaiah 55:11 NIV

CHAPTER 2
GOD APPOINTED MARRIAGE

Loved - but controlled under witchcraft
My one fault in hearing from God was that I did not seek Godly counsel. By plunging into my marriage without counsel, I exposed myself to many hard years which I did not understand. I am going to take the writing that God gave me in October 1989 and place it here for you to read. In this way you can see how powerful this word was and how my spirit received it as truth. I went to this conference with a friend. The conference was at Christian International School of Ministry in Florida headed up by Bill Hammond, a prophetic apostle of faith. The dates of the conference were October 4, 1989 through October 8, 1989. I went with a Christian brother in Christ. Here is the sequence of events that we experienced:

On October 4, 1989, I sat next to James Nastally while in a conference session at Bill Hammond's facility in Florida. My spirit picked up quickly where James was -I was picking up a feeling of disconnection. I even felt uncomfortable sitting next to him. The next day my friend and I bumped into James and his friend at the personalized prophecy session. Again, we sat next to James and his friend. At this time James asked if we would like to go out to lunch with them. I said no, because God had directed me to pray for the conference that evening. But *after the conference, we did go out with James and his friend for coffee. And, as I was sitting across from James the boldness of the Holy Spirit arose in me and I looked at James and said, "You have a real problem."* He looked at me questioningly and said, "What do you mean?" I said, *"You have the inability to feel." He said, "That's my personality",* and I said, *"No, do you want a deliverance, do you want to be set free?" James said yes, and so my*

31

friend and I accompanied James to his motel room. On the way there, we prayed in tongues and God gave us a vision of a detached tree - no sap flowing into the top section of the tree. The Holy Spirit guided us in prayer for James and he was delivered that night from that oppressive spirit. It was beautiful.

On October 7, 1989, while sitting next to James in the conference, *the Lord spoke to me concerning James. He said to me, "This is your appointed spouse." I could not even imagine how this could ever be. We seemed so very different in every way. I asked for a confirmation and the Lord's spirit fell upon me and I began to shake. I said, "Okay, Lord, okay. If you really want this put together then you put it together. I will say nothing to James,* I will not make the first move. I will not give him my phone number or address; you will have to do it all. *Shortly after this, James turned to my friend and I and invited us both to have lunch with them. During lunch he said the Lord was directing him to move to California and that he would like to have our addresses and phone numbers. My mouth almost fell open. Before the luncheon, in the conference, God called James up to the front of the congregation, pulling him out of approximately 600 people in attendance to give him a prophetic word. The word confirmed his calling* that he had been set apart for ministry to serve our Lord Jesus Christ. *That evening, the Lord woke me up at 11:55 p.m. and gave me a prophecy about James and myself.* It was more than I could ever have imagined.

Prophetic words spoken over Jetta personally by God to marry James.
Here is the prophecy God gave me:

"Yea my daughter I have brought you to this hour of your life. It is by my appointment that you have come unto this conference in Florida. *It is by my appointment that I now reveal to you the man I have chosen for you to be equally yoked with to serve My Kingdom and to conqueror the nations.* Think not the journey I have taken you through strange, for you will need the warfare and knowledge of My Spirit that you have gained through these trials for the journey I set before you.

Yea I say to you my daughter, when I revealed to you this morning that this man was to be your husband, My Spirit fell upon you to confirm that these thoughts and this conversation was authentic and from me. I even gave another person insight to see that which I had placed within you both.

Your appointment is great my daughter. *This man has a great calling upon his life, and you are the catalyst needed to bring him into My chosen destiny for his life.* The love I shall give you for this man will be a pure love that will break every shackle the enemy has placed upon this man. It will melt his heart like wax. *You will be a great influence on this man's life and ministry. I shall give you great wisdom and revelation to handle the decisions that lie before you both.* I shall unite you both together and give you one mind in the spirit and you shall flow under My anointed power. I shall take you into nations and I shall set the captives free through your vessels. The arrows of the enemy shall not come near you for My angels are encamped around you. Your commission is a great one. I have prepared you both for this hour. You have waited long and gone through much to obtain the preparation and healings necessary before your uniting. In a little while I will unite you as one. Finish the task that is at hand (master's degree 15-month duration), for you will need the knowledge you will gain from this training. *You will teach My children daughter - and they will learn the secrets I will reveal unto you - secrets for their inner healing which will break the bondages over their lives.*

Do not try to rationalize all and evaluate exactly what you shall do with this degree, only walk in faith child; for I am doing a healing in your mind through this training. The muscles you must exercise will release that which needs releasing. I will impart to you great wisdom and you will be able to be a match for James' great mind. You both will learn much from me. *I will bury My Word deep within your hearts and use it to minister through your vessels to others. My love will flow through your vessels. It will touch the darkness that is before you and illuminate your path.*

Walk in obedience to My Spirit and Word - go forth in My timing. After you have received your training, I will perform great and mighty deeds through your vessels. Your anointed and appointed hour is soon. Wait my daughter, for I have saved you for this hour. Be diligent to accomplish the task before you, for it is a link that will be needed to complete the chain of events in your life - it will be used for My glory. *Proceed dear child in this direction, accomplish the task before you and I will take you before the nations of this land to proclaim My Truth.* I will give you visions and interpretations greater than My servant Daniel. For I have brought the world close - and *you will travel over its distance and proclaim My Words, My Truth, to many lands.* The revelation gifts I shall give you both will surpass Daniel's only in the fact that he traveled one land, you will travel many. *You will do great works in the Name of Jesus Christ, the King of Kings and Lord of Lords."*

You might say, well Jetta, it did not come to pass so this word was not from God.

34

My mistake with James was my insensitivity to his past. When I innocently offended him by something I said, James shut me out of his life and we no longer shared those tender moments through poems. We lost the ability to touch each other's hearts.

I wish to show you the heart of this man so that you can relate to how strong the deceptions of Satan are upon people under witchcraft.

James had a very tender heart. He used to write me love poems. I will include three of these to show you his tender heart.

"THE FATHER'S HOUSE"
POEM BY JAMES S. NASTALLY

Like a diamond in the night,
the Lord has polished you so bright,
Heaven's love has filled you from above,
now you can see the eternal in me,
God dwells not in temples of stone,
but in fragile vessels of flesh and bone.
He has not disdained an eternal abode
but purifies it and calls it gold.
Out of crystal palaces, lovely and light.
He has arisen and banished our night.
He has poured forth His love
and washed us from above,
making an image of Christ
so pure taking away all fear,
gone is man's disgrace,
we are forever locked
in our Father's embrace.
AMEN!

"LOVE IS LIKE"
POEM BY JAMES S. NASTALLY

Love is like a baby's smile which shines brightly for a
while,
Love is like rain drops on a rose petal bejeweled for a
moment then passes quietly away.

Love is like a moonlit night, soft and clear and ever so near,
Love is like an ocean's breeze which blows ever so faintly
through the trees.

Now love is more and greater you see - for long ago a man
hung between Earth and two thieves and poured out His
soul for the ungodly.

Who with supernatural glory and crystalline might, drove
the enemy to everlasting flight.
Who redeeming man brought him back from an Eternal
night.
To an everlasting peace and bright day light.
Now that is love.
AMEN

"ROSES ARE RED & VIOLETS ARE BLUE" POEM BY JAMES S. NASTALLY

Roses are red, and violets are blue,
I can see that Christ has arisen in you.

Gone is Satan's long dark night,
Swallowed up by Christ's eternal light.

The shadows of pain have lost their gain,
For Christ has smashed their evil domain.

As Lazarus of old was called forth from death and the hold
of the Evil One's Breath,

Now sits enthroned in our hearts the matchless love of
Christ never to depart.

Love Divine, Love Divine,
Endless and Eternal Beyond all Time.

AMEN

I have included one poem that I wrote to James so that you can know and feel my heart for this precious man before the poems ceased and our hearts no longer touched one another.

POEM FROM JETTA TO JAMES
December 5, 1990

Riches are grand, but they soon grow old,
A true love who cares, is the treasure to hold.
I love you James my true love who cares and shares!!
You are a prize that Jesus has given unto me,
Soon your health will be restored, and your energy increased.
You'll be blessed because you've held true to your Savior who's the best,
He'll never forsake or leave you, cause you're His very special jewel.
He's polishing you up for His end-time crew,
So, don't be weary for in due season you shall reap the blessing.
You shall know the reason, for your suffering and shame,
And you will burn aglow with Christ's flame.
Your light will flow (His light within you), to a world who will soon know,
That Jesus is their savior, for He paid the price to burn their dross on His cross.
Jesus loves you James and I do too,
You're a real trouper, not a party pooper!!!!

You can see from these poems the heart of this sweet man and, my heart too. As we shared poems together, Christ's love just flowed through us to each other. It was so lovely what we had. So, what happened? I was immature and not sensitive enough to his wounded past. Thus, with boldness,

I one day offended him. He misunderstood what I said one day and from that day on we never touched each other's hearts again.

I paid dearly for my mistake. Although we did not pray together, nor have a typical husband/wife relationship, the closeness we shared through those poems was very real, very bonding, and very deep.

I walked through 24 years of my life with James not understanding God's plan. I just died to my dreams and loved James as a wife should - the best I knew how.

I want to interject here that one must walk through their valley of darkness knowing that God somehow has purpose in it all. I did just that. I gave up my dream and just loved James the best I knew honoring our wedding vows.

God has just recently showed me that James was a seed. He died so that others could live. He was good seed. Although the dream in my heart for his complete healing on Earth never came to pass, God's plan was far greater than mine. The words prophesied to us, that we would win many, many, souls for the kingdom of heaven, are coming to pass as I call them forth. James, now being in the Cloud of Witnesses, is now cleansed of all Earthly hindrances and all the holds of witchcraft he was under have vanished. [Note: James' Earthly father and ex-wife practiced witchcraft.] How glorious is God to honor His Word and to give us grace to carry out the divine mission on Earth that He ordained us to complete for His glory.

God's ways are so different from our ways. I gave up my dream of ministering to the nations so that ALL could come to know and receive Christ as their Savior. I gave up the dream that I would ever be a prophetic voice for the Lord.

I just settled down and loved James the best I knew how. He was very bright and very well read, whereas the only thing I concentrated on was the Word of God. I had little interest in anything else.

James and I lived a simple life. It was isolated from others. There were acquaintances that we met at church, but seldom did we enjoy their companionship in our home. Since my family was out of state and James had lost touch with his family, our families were not part of our lives. James was big on watching Star Trek and other science fiction movies. He also kept himself abreast reading the paper each morning in the bathtub.

James was the owner of two Rottweiler puppies. They were the love of his life. His first dog we called 'Smokey'. He was very friendly and lovable. When Smokey died, James got another Rottweiler. His name was Prince. Unfortunately, when Prince was a puppy another dog attacked him and from then on, he became defensive, aggressive and mean. James was never able to train him properly. We were forced to give him away when he attacked me and bit my arm quite badly. James took me to the emergency hospital where I received medical assistance.

The above is a quick summary of our simple life. It appeared to have no spiritual purpose for God. We essentially walked in solitude with no close friends or family. I did not understand my life with James. I was in a world isolated from others. Although, through it all, I drew very close to God and walked in obedience to His Word. I loved James to the best of my ability and remained a faithful and supportive wife. I share the life of James below with you so that you can understand the severity of the spirit of witchcraft and how it can cripple you from achieving your God given destiny on Earth.

Below is a brief summary of James' qualities.

James was a very conscientious man and after ten years of owning our home, he decided it was time to do some major upkeep and improvements. He then went about refurbishing both the exterior and the interior of our home.

After James had gotten our home all fixed up, painted outside and inside, with new tile floors, I guess God thought I was mature enough in Him to take James home. James collapsed - seemingly having no life in him. The paramedics came and he was taken to the hospital in an ambulance. I was devastated. I called my Pastor, Pastor Michael Constantine, and he came to the hospital with two church members and we all prayed for James's body to be resurrected. At this point he was brain dead but still alive. *Well the Earthly resurrection was not God's plan. Pastor Michael left the room to be alone with God. He asked God why nothing was happening in connection with our prayers and God told him that James did not want to come back. So, I had to release James and let him go. I cannot blame James as he was in such pain and was never able to claim God's Word for himself because he felt he was responsible for his injuries.*

I came home from the hospital after James had passed. When I got into the house I looked straight up to heaven and said to God, "What was this marriage all about?"

That was when God told me that James was received into heaven and placed into the Cloud of Witnesses. I did not even know what the Cloud of Witnesses were. I began to explore the Word and God showed me that the Cloud of

Witnesses consists of special Saints that have passed on and are warring for those on Earth to accomplish His will.

In Robert Henderson's book The Cloud of Witnesses in the Courts of Heaven,[1] he says we are partnering with the Counsel of Heaven (the Cloud of Witnesses) for personal and Kingdom breakthrough.

> *"Therefore, we also,* since we *are surrounded by so great a Cloud of Witnesses,* let us lay aside every weight, and the sin which so easily ensnares us, and let us run with endurance the race that is set before us."[2] (NKJV)

Although James is not present on this Earth, he is very much alive and is in the Cloud of Witnesses in heaven, fighting for the many souls God had promised us. After James departure, God placed in my heart total love and understanding concerning James. Here is the word God gave me:

GOD'S WORD TO JETTA
"You are now one with James: one in mind, one in spirit, one in purpose; no secrets, no deceptions. You need not dig up things of your past. Do not look back. It is very important for your mind to stay on the task at hand. I showed you a vision of your car, it represents your ministry." *God continued "Walk in the spirit at all times - then you will arrive at your spiritual destiny."* He then showed me a vision and I was holding my baby, which was my ministry. He said, "You are out of the reach of the enemy and the world. Remember you are on a vertical with me (meaning God speaks to me directly). Look up to receive your orders and look within your spiritual heart. Although your physical body lives on Earth, your real home

is in heaven. Live from that perspective. You are Mine and I am yours. We are one says the Lord God Almighty."

God had given me a time frame for my training by the Holy Spirit. It turned out to be two years. At that time, He said He would launch me out into the ministry that He had for me to accomplish on Earth - my divine ministry that is written in my Book of Life in heaven.

PROPHECY GIVEN TO JETTA BY PROPHET HENRY JOHNSON

"God always rewards faithfulness. I see you put your hands to the plow. You have submitted yourself under the hand of God. You take complete instructions; you turn to the left; you turn to the right. I'm seeing by June things will be different for you. You will have the provision that God has promised you. Your life will be totally turned around.

God said you are right on course. The things that tried to create havoc and cause problems, God says are no more. This is a brand-new day; you are on a new course with God for the glory of the kingdom of God."

My first outreach is this book. God wants this book published to show people that there is always hope in Him no matter what circumstances you are in or have been through. God can lift you up, out, and above all those clouds of darkness. For Jesus paid the price for you with His precious blood on Calvary. Do not despair. There is coming a miraculous movement of God for the redeemed. His glory cloud will overshadow the darkness that is all about us, and a great breakthrough will manifest for the saints of God. *God just wants to encourage you to stay faithful to His Word to the best of your ability.* He wants you to learn to speak words of life which bring forth God's blessings. *Just praise Him, love Him, and thank Him. Even if you do not feel you have anything to thank Him for, you do. The enemy has just clouded your vision.* Go for a walk in the park, smell the roses, and look at the beautiful trees and flowers. They are all praising God. How much more should we who are created in His image praise Him too?

I truly believe that ALL God showed me when I married James will come to pass. Although James is not here physically with me, he is in the Cloud of Witnesses in heaven fighting for the many souls God promised us. We are still together fighting for those souls to know our Jesus and the power of His resurrection. *God is releasing the supernatural into the Earth unto His redeemed who are tried and found faithful.* So, do not despair. God has not forgotten you. Remember, repentance is a gift, and then comes Godly sorrow. Godly sorrow is simply turning away from your sin and following God's commandments and walking by the Holy Spirit within you. It is repentance, seeing Jesus personally, and recognizing He paid the price for your sins which enables you to pass onto heaven through His blood sacrifice.

May God bless you all with the revelation of truth, of who you are in Christ Jesus, and who He is in you. You carry within you the very same power that Jesus carried when He walked the Earth. He did only what the Father told him to do. When Jesus ascended into heaven, he sent his Holy Spirit, the Comforter, into the hearts of all believers. Jesus sits at the right hand of the Father making intercession for you and me. He sent His Holy Spirit into our hearts to be our mentor. The Holy Spirit speaks to us of what He hears from Father God, and the Son Jesus Christ. The Holy Spirit is the person who brings the glory cloud and brings the anointing that breaks the strongholds in our lives.

"Your Kingdom come, your will be done, on Earth as it is in heaven."[3] (KJV)

"I will surely bless you and make your descendants as numerous as stars in the sky and as the sand on the seashore. Your descendants will take possession of the cities of their enemies"[4] (NIV)

"and through your off-spring all nations on Earth will be blessed, because you have obeyed me."[5] (NIV)

"The tongue has the power of life and death, and those who love it will eat its fruit."[6] (NIV)

"Your words are so powerful that they will kill or give life, and the talkative person will reap the consequences."[7] (TPT)

Watch and be alert for the enemy is always waiting for the opportunity to snare you into his web and steal the destiny God has ordained you to complete on this Earth.

"The thief cometh not, but for to steal, and to kill, and to destroy: I am come that they might have life, and that they might have it more abundantly."[8] (KJV)

End Notes:

1. Henderson, Robert, *The Cloud of Witnesses in the Courts of Heaven*, Destiny Image Publisher, Inc. 2019
2. Hebrews 12:1 NKJV
3. Matthew 6:10 KJV
4. Genesis 22:17 NIV
5. Genesis 22:18 NIV
6. Proverbs 18:21 NIV
7. Proverbs 18:21 TPT
8. John 10:10 KJV

CHAPTER 3
FOUR NEAR DEATH EXPERIENCES

Age 3 (Fell eight feet headfirst into an empty swimming pool)

We live in an imperfect world where we are all exposed to elements beyond our control. When I was just three years old, somehow my mother was not watching my every step. I opened the door of the house, with the pool just a few feet from our home, and I walked over to the pool which was empty. *I leaned over to look at the bottom of that pool and lost my balance - and over I went headfirst. Bang! I hit my head on the hard concrete of that empty pool.* I was blessed not to split my head open. Needless to say, it did some damage and certainly God had his hand on me, or I easily could have permanently injured myself. From that time on, I learned to process my thoughts through my spirit rather than from my intellect. *This led me to live in a world guided by my inner being.* In other words, I had to live by my spirit person (my heart) inside me and not my soul (my intellect). Although at the time I did not know anything about Jesus or about how to walk in the spirit man inside me (my heart); however, *through this experience at this young age, I learned to listen to that inner voice within me.* And as I grew up, I had to depend upon that voice because memorization was extremely difficult for me. I had to be repetitive to retain information in my mind. When I became a Christian, it was difficult to remember scriptures. I had to address scriptures daily repeating them over and over to retain them in my memory. *Through all of this, God had His hand on me. The anointing of God began to fall on me, and I was divinely touched by the Holy Spirit. I began to pray for people and Scriptures would roll out of me. I was praying the Word over people and the anointing of God was there. I could tell when the Spirit of God was upon a person. Through the guidance of the Holy Spirit, I was able to see, in the spirit, the gifts God had placed upon his people. The God in me; the Father, the Son, and the Holy Spirit, was praying and speaking through me. I felt blessed to be used by God in this fashion. It was always my heart's desire to see people happy, set free, and blessed.*

God had much work to do in me though, for I still functioned more in the soul realm (the intellectual mind) than the spiritual realm. I had not completely surrendered my life to God. The Western world teaches us how to function with our intellect and that is how most people walk in this world we live in today.

Below I address the next near-death experience that again changed my life.

Age 28 (Postpartum Depression - 52 shock treatments)
My greatest desire was to have a child. However, it seemed that I was infertile and my chances of having a child were nil. I was desperate and willing to do anything to have this desire of my heart come to pass. I visited a doctor and he told me about a fertility treatment. However, he said if this worked for me, I could have several children at one time. As I mentioned, I was desperate. So, *I took the pills and became pregnant. Carrying my baby went well without any problems. Since I wanted to have a natural birth, I focused on the Lamaze birth system of staring at an object while I was in delivery. What I do remember about my son Kevin's birth is that it was beyond painful. On the scale of 1-20 it was a 22. I was in labor for 28 hours. Kevin was breech* and I needed to have a Cesarean birth; however, Kevin's father (my ex-husband) was not in agreement so that procedure never happened. *Again, the Lord had His hand on both my son Kevin, and myself. Kevin had no brain damage* - which was such a

blessing. In fact, he was born a potential genius. He came from German stock and his grandfather was a genius. His grandfather had the ability to invent just by reading textbooks. He designed several inventions by taking concepts from textbooks and applying the concepts to create different items. He once created a houseboat with an opening that you could stare down and see fish through. You could actually fish from this opening. Another invention and concept he developed was the machinery to burn and re-fire charcoal to re-energize it. He was then able to sell this activated charcoal to the public at a reduced price.

Poppa Ted, Kevin's grandfather, was such a fun person. He was full of life, full of energy, and very giving towards his family and friends. To this day I miss that sweet man who blessed us all so much.

It was not long after Kevin's birth that I became ill. I went into serious postpartum depression - so much so that my husband sent my son and I to my parents' home in Fallbrook, California. We had been living at the time in Berkeley, California - near the University of Berkeley. *My mother was very caring and was wonderful with Kevin. She sought professional help for me; however, she was not a practicing Christian and lacked discernment. She chose a mental hospital in Encinitas, California. In those days they treated postpartum depression with electrical shock treatments. The doctor that treated me was an atheist that denied the existence of God.*

These electrical shock treatments erased memory. The shock treatments were so potent that they had to place a cloth inside my mouth so that I would not bite my tongue off. Truly, they did erase my memory. I essentially became a vegetable. My sister came and visited me every day.

When I recovered, my sister would often tell me how totally zoned out from this world I was. One day she came into my room and pulled my hair, with no reaction. She picked up my legs one by one and they dropped like lead weights. I was totally nonfunctional. She did the same with my arms and they flapped at my side. In other words, my various body parts acted as if they were not connected.

She told me that when she left the room that day she cried out to God: "God either fix her or take her home." At that time, my sister knew of God but did not have a personal relationship with Jesus. But God heard her prayer. For you see, God loves all of us and knows our hearts and wishes all to be saved and come to know truth. So, the next time my sister came to visit, I was sitting up in bed. I immediately said to her, "Where have you been sis?" She was shocked. She said, "Me, where have you been? You've been clocked out of reality and now you are back." At this time, I had received around 48 shock treatments. I proceeded to tell my sister, Sandy, what had happened to me. I said, "Jesus came and visited me in the night. He is nothing like I had imagined Him to be. He was a brilliant blaze of light. I could see His face, but He was totally in the Shekinah Glory. His presence was the illumination of true light and truth. He spoke to me about my destiny in Him. He told me what my ministry for Him was, and then He deposited into my spirit all that He had told me. It was awesome. *I learned I had a purpose; I learned the direction of my destiny. He deposited His love within my heart, and I have never been the same since that day.* To know that all things work together for the good of those that love God is a remarkable revelation that we cannot fathom in our intellectual mind (our soul realm).

"And we know that all things work together for good to them that love God, to them who are the called according to His purpose."[1] (KJV)

After my visitation with Jesus, the doctor truly thought I was crazy. Although she could see that I was no longer a mental vegetable, she proceeded to continue the shock treatments. *She gave me approximately four more shock treatments. In so doing, she erased my mind's conscious recollection of my visitation with Jesus.* However, she was never able to take me back to that vegetable state again for God had deposited light and truth into my spirit. *I never was touched mentally again by those shock treatments.* It is an amazing gift to walk in the spirit. To be guided by the light of Christ. It is an inward witness within your spirit.

"In Him was life; and the life was the light of men."[2] (KJV)

(Please note that all the information concerning my shock treatments were given to me by my sister). *My experience with my visitation with Jesus in the Encinitas, California hospital was related to me in 1990 when my sister came to visit. I had no recollection in my mind of anything my sister related to me when she spoke of this incident. [Although my mind did not retain any of this, my spirit did, and I followed out the will of God for my life by following the voice of my spirit within me.]*

Breast Cancer Surgery, October 2, 2010
My cousin shared with me her experience with breast cancer. It was very serious and because of this I decided to have a breast mammogram. I was opposed to having a mammogram because I had read, according to doctors practicing natural nutrition, that mammograms were

dangerous and generally did more harm to the body than good. *It had been 12 years since my last mammogram.*

Well I decided to go for a mammogram. The results of my mammogram showed foreign objects in my breast. It showed a lump was there, and that it was not a bubble that could be broken off. It took several days to get back the results from the biopsy. The results showed that I did indeed have a tumor and that it had to be removed. My husband, James, went with me for all my appointments. He really suffered waiting for the results of all those tests. After surgery, they again sent the biopsy samples for further testing and found it had gone into my lymph nodes. Therefore, *I had to go for full radiation treatments which lasted for six weeks.* I was also working full time while these treatments were going on. I was given great favor with my boss.

During the last week of radiation, I felt very weak. I had almost no strength and energy left in my body. I knew my immune system was very low. Therefore, I watched where I went and what I ate very carefully.

I was referred to an oncologist who wanted me to go through chemotherapy; but my radiologist said there was no need for this, so I rejected that procedure. However, I did go on their prescribed cancer pills which played havoc with my system. Those pills had severe side effects which created many uncomfortable symptoms. *For over a year I was on those pills and finally, I decided to fight this by diet and natural vitamins. I sought out every natural remedy I could find health wise and learned a lot about eating habits, vitamins, and nutrition.*

I was able to pull my system back into order so that I once again became healthy and vibrant.

I say thank you Jesus! This indeed could have eliminated me but God and His grace and mercy, and His hand of love were upon me. *Once again, God spared me from death. Had I not acted upon the information my cousin sent me and gone for a mammogram, I could easily have been taken out by the devil.*

Scammed after death of my husband - ended up in Psychiatric ward.

After James passed, I worked at getting all my legal matters in order. First, I compiled a power of attorney over my accumulated assets; then I assigned a medical authorization over my health. These actions proved essential for addressing Satan's next attack on me.

Now Satan will always try to keep you from obtaining God's blessings and fulfilling your destiny. He will enter in through some void in your life. This is exactly what happened to me.

I was scammed (conned) through a void that I did not even realize I had – the desire to be loved by a man. This occurred a few years after my husband James was received into heaven. I include the particular details of being scammed later in this book along with actions readers can take to avoid such an experience.

After I was scammed, I nearly died as I suffered complete loss of my mental faculties. My brain had ceased functioning normally and I was placed in a psychiatric hospital. I was there for six weeks and the doctors believed it was very unlikely that I would ever fully recover my mental faculties.

Had it not been for the prayers of many of God's chosen intercessors and my family and friends, I believe I never would have recovered. Praise God for the prayers of the saints and of my family! God miraculously healed me! The road back was not easy; but, through perseverance and much help from my son, my sister, and dear friend Jeannie, I recovered.

Because of God's grace, the prayers of saints, and my dear sister who knows my calling, along with my son's love for me, the devil was not successful. *That is why people get scammed, because there is a void in their life somewhere - a crack that the enemy slips through to bring destruction to them.*

I now have completely surrendered my life to God. When I finally came to the end of Jetta and surrendered all of my life to Him, He brought back my dream. In fact, He brought it back so strongly that I know it will happen.

I understand now who I am in Christ, and who He is in me. I now understand the power of the Father, the Son, and the Holy Spirit that reside in me. My commission is simply to obey what the Holy Spirit tells me to do. This requires standing in the midst of almost impossible situations and continuing to stand in faith until God manifests what He has shown me into the Earthly realm. That is exactly what King David did in his Psalms in the Bible. He would state how impossible the situation was and then he would praise the Lord that His Word was true, and that He would deliver him from the enemy's traps. David learned to sing the Word of God which is incredibly powerful as David always came out victorious.

God wants this message of hope to penetrate the hearts of the hopeless. He wants to show you how mighty and powerful He is - and that if His chosen vessels will hold onto His Word, even though their dreams have died, in the end He will resurrect them all.

Through my healing process, God showed me that I got caught up in this scam situation because I had resentment and bitterness in my heart towards James because he was not able to show his Earthly love to me through embraces of love and tenderness as this link in our marriage was missing. I had unforgiveness towards him and the enemy saw that crack, that opening, and entered into my soul. After God revealed this to me, I repented of the bitterness and resentment I had towards James.

Growing in God is not easy. It is like peeling an onion, one layer at a time. God tries so hard to bring us into His spiritual realm, out of the soul realm. With good intentions we often go amiss. Mixing the spirit realm with the soul realm (intellect) does not work. So, God allows us to go through our trials before we give Him everything and that is exactly what happened to me.

During my 24 years of marriage, I lost all my discernment and spiritual gifts when I placed myself under my husband's authority. These gifts only came back to me when God delivered me from the spirit of witchcraft.

I can only say that through perseverance, diligence, and obedience to what the Holy Spirit directed me to do, I came through to another realm in the Lord. He lifted me above my circumstances and provided for all my needs. He now instructs me daily in the direction I am to go. His vision is so clear in my heart that I know it will come to pass.

God has given me the ministry of a seer. One who sees in the spirit and calls the spiritual things into the physical

Earthly realm. Just as Abraham was tested in his faith, we all must be tested too so that God can trust us with His power and authority on Earth - to speak His will into the Earth. *We must be cloaked in humility. We are willing servants yielded to His spirit to activate His will on Earth as it is in heaven. You are now sons of God* (Galatians 4:6-7). *Pride cannot be a factor in your lives.* It is the very thing that caused Satan to fall from heaven - stay humble.

END NOTES:
1. Romans 8:28 KJV
2. John 1:4 KJV

CHAPTER 4
JAMES HONORED AT HIS MEMORIAL SERVICE

James Nastally, my husband for 24 years, died on June 19, 2014 and now resides in heaven. He is part of the Cloud of Witnesses, fighting the spiritual battle to win souls to the Truth, the person of Jesus Christ.

God honored James with a very special and anointed memorial service on June 24, 2014. Our church family and neighborhood acquaintances attended, as well as his best friend of many years, who travelled from Omaha, Nebraska with his wife to attend.

Psalms 1 – The way of the righteous and the wicked
"Blessed is the man that walketh not in the counsel of the ungodly, nor standeth in the way of sinners, nor sitteth in the seat of the scornful."[1] (KJV)
"But his delight is in the law of the LORD; and in His law doth he meditate day and night."[2] (KJV)
"And he shall be like a tree planted by the rivers of water, that bringeth forth his fruit in his season; his leaf also shall not wither; and whatsoever he doeth shall prosper."[3] (KJV)
"The ungodly are not so: but are like the chaff which the wind driveth away."[4] (KJV)
"Therefore, the ungodly shall not stand in the judgment, nor sinners in the congregation of the righteous."[5] (KJV)
"For the LORD knoweth the way of the righteous: but the way of the ungodly shall perish".[6] (KJV)

SONGS:

These were the three songs sung at James' memorial by Denee Ibert. Denee spontaneously showed up, directed by God, to sing these beautiful songs for my James. She carried the anointing and it permeated the entire atmosphere with the presence of God.

"Victory in Jesus" [7]
"The Old Rugged Cross" [8]
"In the Garden" [9]

"Victory in Jesus" (written by E. M. Bartlett)
I heard an old, old story, how a Savior came from glory
How He gave His life on Calvary to save a wretch like me
I heard about His groaning, of His precious blood's atoning
Then I repented of my sins and won the victory

Chorus:
Oh victory in Jesus, my Savior forever
He sought me and He bought me with His redeeming blood
He loved me 'ere I knew Him and all my love is due Him
He plunged me to victory beneath the cleansing flood

I heard about His healing, of His cleansing power revealing
How He made the lame to walk again and He caused the
blind to see - and then I cried, "Dear Jesus, come and heal
my broken spirit". I then obeyed His blest command and
gained the victory

I heard about a mansion He has built for me in glory
And I heard about the streets of gold beyond the crystal sea
About the angels singing and the old redemption story
Oh and some sweet day I'll sing up there the song of
victory

"The Old Rugged Cross" (written by George Bernard)
On a hill far away, stood an old rugged Cross
The emblem of suffering and shame
And I love that old Cross where the dearest and best
For a world of lost sinners was slain

So, I'll cherish the old rugged Cross
Till my trophies at last I lay down
I will cling to the old rugged Cross
And exchange it some day for a crown
Oh, that old rugged Cross so despised by the world
Has a wondrous attraction for me
For the dear Lamb of God, left His Glory above
To bear it to dark Calvary

So, I'll cherish the old rugged Cross
Till my trophies at last I lay down
I will cling to the old rugged Cross
And exchange it some day for a crown

In the old rugged Cross, stained with blood so divine
A wondrous beauty I see
For the dear Lamb of God, left His Glory above
To pardon me

"In the Garden" (written by Van Morrison)
I come to the garden alone
While the dew is still on the roses
And the voice I hear, falling on my ear
The Son of God discloses
And He walks with me
And He talks with me
And He tells me I am His own
And the joy we share as we tarry there
None other has ever known

He speaks and the sound of His voice
Is so sweet the birds hush their singing
And the melody that He gave to me
Within my heart is ringing
And He walks with me
And He talks with me
And He tells me I am His own
And the joy we share as we tarry there
None other has ever known

PROPHETIC POEM:
Below is a prophetic poem written by prophet Llewellyn David McDaniel, who was James' friend.

"The vine and the branches and the twig, the least than and the least in the House of God. Oh, the twig that Father God has called and chosen me to be. A fragile one and a weak one, as considered by some, but not to My Father who strengthens me.

For as the winds of His Spirit begin to blow, I hear Him gently say unto me,

Oh, little twig be strong and walk on for I will cause thee to walk with Me from glory to glory.

So, fear not, for you are not alone for you were predestined by me throughout the annuls of time to sit alongside the vine and the branch upon My throne for all of eternity."

James Steven Nastally's Life Story -
Read by his wife, Jetta, at his memorial:

James had a difficult life on Earth. He came from an alcoholic and abusive home. He was abandoned by his natural father, at a very early age. (Note: His father practiced witchcraft.) This affected him deeply. He essentially became a recluse after the departure of his father. He removed himself from people and started reading books as well as devouring knowledge within encyclopedias. In 1967 James was drafted into the US Navy. After the Navy he returned to Detroit, Michigan where his family resided. *He never had the opportunity to go on to college, but like Abraham Lincoln he was self-taught through the reading of books and encyclopedias.*

When James came to the Lord, slowly but surely, God worked His love for him into His heart. He developed a deep compassion for people in need. He learned to discern through the Holy Spirit those who were truly in need. James became a man transformed by the renewing of his mind.

At the time of his death, James had read the Old Testament at least 300 times, and the New Testament more than 1,000 times. He was a man of the Word. He was a man who knew world history. He could put things together and discern the signs of the time.

James learned compassion for his fellow man through his sufferings. He had deep health issues which he never complained about because he felt he had caused them by his foolishness of not listening to his body signs (he had body twitches). He had been warned by doctors and professional body trainers to stop lifting heavy weights. By not listening to good counsel, he caused severe nerve damage to his body and he was constantly in pain from it. His family had a genetic history of high blood pressure. *During the last year of James' life, he took high blood pressure medication. He went beyond his limitations; the stress was too much for his body and he went into hypertension, he lost consciousness and his heart and pulse stopped.*

God in his mercy felt it time to take James home. It took me 24 years of marriage to James before God felt I was ready to walk through life without a mate. What I learned from James was structure, consistency, and obedience - and so many other attributes. I learned the patience of God, and the love of God, through the trial of this marriage.

Truly James gained compassion for his fellow man through his sufferings. He did not display a lot of emotions, but his caring heart was deeply concerned about the state of another person's health and welfare.

He demonstrated Christ-like love to others through his actions and deeds. He mowed the neighbor's lawn regularly because she had no husband and had 4 children. *He witnessed through his actions, deeds and by example to show the love of God to mankind.*

A TESTIMONY OF GOD'S LOVE AND MERCY

Even though I never witnessed this part of James, when he was received up into heaven friends and neighbors came to honor him for his deeds and works that touched many of their hearts. James sowed the seed of God's love to others.

James was an instrument of God. When God called James into His presence, he left a legacy, his seed, and it was planted into the ground to bring forth the harvest. God is now taking James' legacy seed and opening the eyes of the blind using it to bring forth souls into the kingdom of God.

God has purpose in all that He does. He loves everyone and wishes all to come to Him.

James witnessed in action and deeds the love of Christ in his own way. He felt that for people to really receive and understand the love of Jesus Christ, that Christ Himself had to open the door of their heart. Therefore, James did not witness by telling people about Christ in the flesh. Only when the Spirit of God and His anointing was on him did he speak, then and only then he felt that those anointed words would penetrate the heart to whom the Word was spoken.

For Jesus Christ is the truth, the way, and the life according to **John 14:6** in the Bible. He opened the door to eternal life for all of us who will embrace Him as our Lord and Savior. He paid a huge price with His blood to redeem us back to Father God. Originally, mankind had an intimate relationship with God and that is what we were created to have on Earth with Him. God came daily to fellowship with His creations, Adam and Eve, in the Garden of Eden. God had provided for all their needs before He even created them.

But after the fall of man, all mankind inherited a sin nature as did their bloodlines. Adam and Eve lost that open communication they shared with God in the Garden of Eden. God had to send them out of the Garden of Eden because they had disobeyed him and eaten of the forbidden tree of the knowledge of good and evil.

The devil came and tempted Eve with a lie that sounded to the ear so true and good. He deceived her and twisted what God had said, causing her to doubt the truth. He whispered into her ear the lie that God did not want her to eat the fruit because He did not want her to be like Him. He planted a seed of doubt into her spirit that her God was withholding something beautiful from her, something she actually already had received and did not know. In fact,

God had given Adam and Eve rule over everything in the garden (**Genesis 2:15-17**) *and had created mankind to have dominion over the Earth and everything in it* (**Genesis 1:26-28**). *They were created in God's very own image and likeness. They were free to partake of everything except one thing: the tree of knowledge of good and evil* (**Genesis 2:9**). That was restricted for their protection. He clearly spoke this to Adam, although it is unclear if Adam relayed this to Eve.

Before the fall of Adam and Eve, *Satan was a beautiful anointed cherub in heaven. When he was thrown out of heaven for the sin of pride and trying to exalt himself above God, he lost all his beauty. And in the garden, he took the form of a speaking serpent to deceive mankind. He approached Eve with his cunning lies and deceptions.*

Eve embraced and received the lies told to her by Satan as truth. For she looked with her eyes and saw the fruit to be beautiful. Satan had told her that this fruit would make her wise. She then took the fruit, disobeying the instructions of God, and ate it. Pride and lust had entered into her being. Adam was beside her when this occurred, and he said nothing to her. He was her covering, he had the authority to correct her, but he did nothing. As Eve quickly passed the fruit to Adam, he partook of it disregarding God's commandment to him. Eve was deceived but Adam willingly chose to disobey God.

This is the same way Satan works in people today: withholding from mankind, the disastrous end results of their sin through following the lust of their eyes. One cannot go against the word of God and His commandments and expect to be blessed.

Originally, both Adam and Eve were cloaked with God's glory and they had no need for Earthly clothes for the glory of God covered them. However, after they ate of the forbidden fruit both of their eyes were opened and they knew they were naked. They lost their spiritual covering of God's glory and fear and shame entered their being. *Before Adam took and tasted of the forbidden fruit, he had no consciousness of sin - he was Christ-like, holy.* So, Adam and Eve lost their innocence and they took on the sin nature of Satan. Sin had now separated both of them from God and their close fellowship with Him. *Then God, for the protection of mankind, removed both Adam and Eve from the beautiful Garden of Eden. He did this because had they eaten of the fruit of the tree of life, mankind would have eternally remained in the state of sin and there would be no way back to their Creator, God Almighty. For in their sin, they had erected a wall between themselves and God (and the blessing God placed upon them became a curse). Their soul and their spirit were now separated.* In fact, their spirits were no longer alive to God. They could now only walk in the soul realm, for mankind is made up of spirit, soul, and body. The soul is your emotions, your intellect, and your will. Mankind, was never created for death, disease, or lack. Through the disobedient act of Adam and Eve, mankind became the slave of Satan who brings death and destruction to all who listen to his lies.

BUT GOD had a redemptive plan for mankind before the foundation of the Earth. It was through the sacrificial atoning blood of Jesus Christ that He could redeem mankind back to Himself. However, Jesus had to agree to be the redeeming sacrifice. He had a choice, He could choose to be the sacrifice and redeem mankind, or He could say no to God. He chose to be obedient to God's desire and design for His life. He was willing and obedient. *This is why the virgin birth occurred. There had to be purity of*

65

blood without a sin nature. Jesus was immaculately conceived by the power of the Holy Spirit in the womb of Mary. But Mary too had to agree and accept this immaculate conception. When the angel Gabriel came to her announcing that she would be impregnated, she said, "How can it be that I could conceive for I have known no man." She did not understand. And *the angel Gabriel told her that the Holy Spirit would fall upon her and impregnate her. Then Mary said, "Let it be unto me according to thy word"* (**Luke 1:38**). Father God had to have the Holy Spirit fall upon a human being, a willing vessel, in order to redeem mankind back to Himself.

God created man even though He knew that he would fall. God wanted relationship with mankind. By Adam's disobedience, he essentially sold mankind out to the devil and we took on the nature of sin. Jesus Christ came and paid the price to buy us back to God. He redeemed us with His untainted holy blood. He redeemed us back to Father God by His precious and pure blood on the Cross of Calvary.

This is the story of God's love for His precious people whom He created to be His family. He sent His Son, who had to be willing to come to Earth and become a human sacrifice for the sins of mankind. For only through His pure and redemptive blood could this be possible.

While on Earth, Jesus did only what the Father told Him to do and no more. He never impulsively reached out to the needy unless directed to do so by the Father. He lived a life of purity and goodness on this Earth. And for that the devil planted in the minds of the evil rulers His crucifixion. They falsely accused Him of sinning.

History has a way of repeating itself. When people disregard the rules of life that God outlined for us to live by in the Holy Bible, when they write their own ticket, eventually, they fall into deep sin and mankind again repeats history.

May the Holy Spirit fill all your hearts with the truth of Jesus Christ. These times are tainted with the minds of evil men. We must learn to walk under the anointing and the umbrella of God's Word. We must hear what we are to do through the Holy Spirit. This can only be when you surrender your soul unto God and walk in His truth. Then indeed you will do only what the Father, the Son, and the Holy Spirit direct you to do.

Praise God that He is able, but we must be drawn by His truth, and our eyes must be open to receive His truth. For *Jesus is the truth, the way, and the life. He is interceding for us all at the right hand of the Father in heaven. He is omnipresent - everywhere at once. Embrace Him, lift your heart to Him and accept Him as your savior. He is our gateway back to the Father. Heaven is real and so is hell.*

"Come, come quickly", says the Father, "for My hand will bring judgment upon the Earth for its violence and its disobedience to My Word." Open your heart and receive the sacrifice that Christ paid for you by His blood shed on Calvary. Embrace Him as your Savior today.

He will show you truth, He will show you love, He will purge your soul of all its impurities. He wants to give you the "God Nature" which is 'LOVE'.

Thank you, Lord Jesus, for giving all mankind a chance to come back to the creator of the universe - God Almighty. We praise You for Your goodness, for Your caring, for

Your love. For You are well able to take a people and transform them into Your image so that righteousness can prevail once again in our land.

End Notes:
1. Psalms 1:1 KJV
2. Psalms 1:2 KJV
3. Psalms 1:3 KJV
4. Psalms 1:4 KJV
5. Psalms 1:5 KJV
6. Psalms 1:6 KJV
7. "Victory in Jesus"-by E.M Bartlett.
8. "The Old Rugged Cross" - by George Bernard
9. "In the Garden" by Van Morrison

CHAPTER 5

DEATH OF THE SOUL -
COMPLETE SURRENDER TO GOD

Through my experiences, especially my last one where I was truly scammed out of all my money, I have, through perseverance, consistency, faithfulness, and diligence, sought the Lord each day for His divine will. I now know what my calling is in Him. And *because I have surrendered all to God and my vessel is now His, I am a servant ready and willing to speak His Words into the atmosphere to bring His will to pass on this Earth.* In this process of dying to my soul, and having Jesus reign and rule in my person, I have lost all desire for Earthly goods.

The desire of my heart is to give my gifts, talents, labor and resources unto the kingdom of God, as the Holy Spirit directs, so that people will know truth - that hell and heaven are real places. Without repentance of sins and acceptance of Jesus, people will enter the gates of hell, a place of eternal torment.

The vision God has given me is immense. God spoke to me when I married James that many souls would be won into the kingdom of heaven through our vessels. I now can believe Him for that word. It is only through His Word and the knowledge of His truth that people are touched. You cannot sit and debate with people situations and differences that are contrary to the bible - they will simply not listen.

During these two years of preparation, being hidden away with the Holy Spirit to learn the language of the Holy Spirit, I have had two occasions to see His Word change people. I was only a vessel to be used to speak out what the Holy Spirit told me to speak, and in so doing, miracles came forth. God's anointing came forth. The Holy Spirit brought the presence of the Shekinah Glory into the atmosphere and people were transformed. No one had to preach to them, they were transformed simply by His presence. *Over 47 years ago, Dick Mills gave me a prophetic word that penetrated my heart and has stayed with me for all these years.* That word is found in **Psalms 30:5** (KJV).

> *"For His anger endureth but a moment, in His favour is life; weeping may endure for a night but joy cometh in the morning. "*[1] (KJV)

I also received another scriptural prophecy that same year stating God would put a new heart in me: A heart of flesh - His heart of love.

Ezekiel 36:26-27 (KJV)

"A new heart also will I give you, and a new spirit will I put within you: and I will take away the stony heart out of your flesh, and I will give you a heart of flesh."[2] (KJV)
"And I will put My spirit within you, and cause you to walk in My statutes, and ye shall keep My judgments and do them."[3] *(KJV)*

This is exactly what has happened to me. God removed my stony heart and gave me His heart. A heart of compassion and love for all His creations.

I now can truly say my mourning has passed - God's joy has truly come upon me. All the promises of God are ours when we claim them in faith. When we travel through our fire, and pass the tests, we are elevated above the enemy. God takes us to another level in Him. We are able to see from God's perspective. We are truly not of this world. Our home is in heavenly places in Christ Jesus. We know who we are in Him, and who He is in us. And there is no weapon formed against us that can prosper.

"For the weapons of our warfare are not carnal, but mighty through God to the pulling down of strong holds;"[4] (KJV)

This is not to say you will not have warfare. In fact, warfare is increased to beyond what one can imagine.

I received eleven prophetic words that everything stolen from me would be restored with interest. (These were prophetic words I received from established Apostles, Prophets, Evangelists, Pastors, and teachers.) However, I had an inner witness that for these words to come to pass I would need to watch the words of my mouth and speak, think, imagine, and feel, only what was holy and righteous according to God's Word. I had to decide to walk the way of the Word in order to inherit these blessings. The intents of my heart had to line up with God's Word.

Needless to say, I surrendered everything to God. It was a long trial, fighting the devil with nothing but faith and calling the invisible things forth to appear in the Earthly realm. And I kept seeing God clear my slate, repeatedly. It was a miraculous journey which I am still on. I have truly learned the power of God's Word and the power of faith - God's faith.

Through the Holy Spirit mentoring me through all my trials, I saw the hand of God go out on my behalf to clear my slate and set me free. Learning the language of the Holy Spirit is so important for all of God's redeemed and also for the lost. He loves everyone. He wants to draw us all into His loving arms and heal all our wounds and sufferings.

Yes, I was scammed out of all my money and savings, but God allowed it all so that Jetta would die and relinquish her body and soul to the Holy Spirit. It really was the death of my soul. I completely surrendered everything to God, and He turned my life around. I had tried so hard to help others and everything I did went amiss. One cannot help another through a mixture of spirit and soul (soul: an act of intellectual reasoning.) One must totally submit and surrender to God, dying to his or her own self will and surrendering to God's will. In doing this, you become a vessel that God can use to win souls into His Kingdom. You learn to listen, hear, and activate the instructions given to you by the Holy Spirit. It really is a faith walk. You know who you are in Christ and you learn how to recognize the voice of the Holy Spirit.

To learn to receive from the Holy Spirit, you must walk in God's faith. He speaks to you through an inner witness. You cannot name it and claim it unless it is given to you by the Holy Spirit. *It must be the will of God - His will, not your will. If it is in the Word of God, it is His will.* God's timing is perfect. He is not too late, and He is not too early. Although you might feel totally overwhelmed by your circumstances, totally defeated, and totally useless, God really is in control. *He has set a fire under you and that fire will burn all the impurities from your soul. He will light your fire with His glory if you will trust Him and walk according to His Word. Walk according to His Spirit within you trusting Him with all your heart.*

You must have a vision in front of you of where you are going with the Lord - of what your Earthly destiny is for Him. And when you obtain this and walk in the light of His Word, the devil is no match for you - for greater is He that is within you than he that is within the world.

SUMMARY
Complete surrender to God is required to totally walk in and use the authority that God has given the born-again believer. You must walk by the Spirit of God listening to the voice of the Holy Spirit within yourself. (Note: this voice will sound like your own voice). To stay free from Satan's deceptions, you must obey the word of God.

Learning to praise God through everything that happens to you is a process. I get amazed at times when something is broken that I used to think was so important such as crystal pieces or heirlooms which had great sentimental value at one time - now they all seem so insignificant. It's as if I have no negative reaction. I can actually praise God through it all without anger arising in me. Now that's real growth. *You can measure your growth in Christ by your trials. Are you dead yet? Dead people don't react. When your soul realm (your flesh) is dead you can go through trials with thanksgiving.*

Your growth in God depends upon you listening and activating the instructions given to you by the Holy Spirit within your person. It depends upon YOU, how hungry you are for the things of God. When you surrender all to Him, you grow rapidly. And when you can come through your trials victoriously, God will elevate you to another level in Him. With this authority in Christ Jesus, the devil is now under your feet. You know who you are in Christ Jesus and the authority He has given you over the devil.

This walk with God is an exciting venture. *Writing this book has been challenging for me. Sometimes being obedient to God is not easy nor pleasing to our flesh. It was never my heart's desire to expose my personal life to the world. But by showing my failures and successes to others, faith and hope can flood your souls. Yes, there is*

73

light at the end of the tunnel. It is through our many trials that we are purged and set free from our soul realm. Through our personal fires of tribulation, we have been set free by the blood of the Lamb (Jesus) to intercede for the lost.

A Unified Church brings forth Truth and restoration to the lost.

Faith is not inherited, it is shared.

God is reaching down and inviting you to be a member of His family. He loves you so much. If He can take someone as simple as myself, for the Word says He takes the foolish to confound the wise, then I believe He can use anyone whose heart reaches out to Him in truth. *Each of us have different gifts that God has placed within us. That is why when we come together in a church body and have unity in the spirit, He uses every one of us to bring us into a corporate anointing. The physical body has parts or members such as fingers, arms, legs, eyes, ears, nose, and toes and they each have a function. Each has a purpose and when one is injured, the whole body suffers.*

For example, I accidentally caught my baby toe on an object which damaged it greatly. At first, I thought I had broken it. Afterwards it turned this awful color of black and blue. At that point I could hardly walk. Now that is just a baby toe. I could not wear shoes, and I could not walk correctly. It took almost two weeks before I could wear shoes again. After this toe was healed, it never looked the same. It had taken on a new shape. It was puffy and fat. This is similar in the Body of Christ. When one is injured, all are affected. The injury causes a deformation of the original look of the body. However, something has taken hold and God is using the change for His glory in order to bring forth unity and servitude to His church body.

We are changed into a metamorphosis state like that of a caterpillar changing into a butterfly. The Lord transforms us into His image using all our trials to bring us into unity and love for the brethren. That is what He is seeking. A church body that is in unity and harmony with Him to proclaim His Word throughout the land - bringing the unseen forth by decreeing and declaring it into existence.

Look into your heart. What lays within your heart? What thoughts and impressions keep coming to your mind? *What is the true desire of your heart? The message is there in your heart. God has placed gifts within you. He wants your gifts (the gift of light and life within you) to be released into the darkness that surrounds the atmosphere of Earth.*

When your gifts of light and life surface they will lead souls into the kingdom of God. My inner gift and desire of my heart was always to see the hopeless and abused delivered from their despair and brought to the truth of Jesus Christ. The fire I went through to get my heart's desire, purged my flesh of many impurities. I shall indeed see the many souls won for God's kingdom that were promised to James and I. Without God's divine plan, and His hand of mercy and grace upon my life, this could never have happened. God is using all the sequence of events that I went through for His glory and has transformed me into His vessel of light. Apart from the Body of Christ praying for me, and the revelation that He gave my sister and son to hold onto the unseen and grasp and speak the Word forth for my full recovery, I would never have made it. God found a way and released His faith through His people in intercessory prayer so I could fulfill my Earthly destiny. Truly God's ways are miraculous.

I am so encouraged that as you read these words, God's faith is being imparted into your soul - that you are grasping who you are in Him, that God loves you so much that He has kept you for these end times, and that through His Son, Jesus Christ, you have been redeemed and set free. You have only to embrace Him as your savior and follow His commandments. There is so much hope for the hopeless and the distraught - for with God all things are possible.

I challenge you to hand your life over to Jesus, to accept His free gift of eternal life of goodness, mercy, grace, and righteousness - to embrace Him with all your heart and to lean not to your own understanding but in all your ways follow Him as He guides you into His blessings. It is an exciting journey unlike anything you've ever gone through before.

Remember, He loves you more than you can comprehend. The fullness of His love is incomprehensible to our human minds.

You are a blessing; you all are His chosen vessels. Release yourselves into your destiny and go forward to conquer the land for Jesus Christ who died to set the captives free.

> *"Ye are of God, little children, and have overcome them: because greater is He that is in you, than he that is in the world."* [5] (KJV)

GOD IS LOVE, and you are His messengers of love on this Earth to share truth to a lost world.

> "Beloved, let us love one another: for love is of God; and everyone that loveth is born of God, and knoweth God."[6] (KJV)

"Come" says Father God, "sit at my table and have supper with Me. Remember there is nothing too hard for Me. I created the Earth and the heavens, and My hand is outstretched over them all. Come, come to My table where there is provision for your every need."

End Notes:
1. Psalm 30:5 KJV
2. Ezekiel 36:26 KJV
3. Ezekiel 36:27 KJV
4. 2 Corinthians 10:4 KJV
5. I John 4:4 KJV
6. I John 4:7 KJV

JETTA NASTALLY

CHAPTER 6
APPOINTED MISSION TRIPS

Below I shall share God's miracles that occurred on a voyage at sea where God miraculously healed members of my adopted family and set them free through the power of HIS Word. Christ touched and healed His people. I spoke what the Holy Spirit directed and witnessed His anointing power flowing through me to this family.

Listed below are the members of Jeannie (Eugenia) Ranney's family. We all boarded the Carnival Breeze Cruise ship for a 7-day Caribbean venture in late February 2018.

1. Jeannie Ranney (Eugenia)
2. Bailey and Brenda Lizarraga and their two girls Eliza and Isabel
3. Bernardo (Benny) and Monette Lizarraga
4. Noah and Tatum Lizarraga
5. Jason Daugherty (adopted family member)
6. Myself: Jetta Nastally

God's angels worked mightily to bring forth miracles on this divinely appointed cruise. I will recap these miracles and write in detail the work that the Holy Spirit and the angels of God did for this family - it was awesome! All miracles were done in the Name of Jesus Christ.

Day 1
Miracle #1
Benny's (Jeannie's son-in-law) back was out, and he was suffering considerable pain caused by his sciatica nerve. Benny asked for me to pray for him. (Using the Frances and Charles Hunter and Joan Hunter Ministries techniques I began to pray and proceed.) I first had Benny extend his

*arms out towards me to check and see if they were the same
length. They were not; one hand was about an inch shorter
than the other. His legs were also off about an inch. After
prayer, both arms and legs grew out to match the length of
their corresponding limb. All this was done by the
anointing of the mighty Holy Spirit in the Name of Jesus
Christ. Jesus is the healer; we are only His servants.*

*However, the sciatica nerve was still causing Benny
considerable pain and discomfort. I asked the Holy Spirit
what to do and He said to place my hand on his leg area
and command the pain to stop in the Name of Jesus Christ.
I was obedient and did so and the pain completely went
away.* Thank you, thank you Father God, Lord Jesus, and
mighty Holy Spirit. *That pain was gone forever and has
never returned to this day.*

Day 3
Miracle #2
The first port we arrived at was Montego Bay, Jamaica.
*We went to a wonderful beach and we were ready to swim
in this beautiful sky-blue water. However, Brenda
(Jeannie's daughter-in-law) was terrified of the water and
she did not know how to swim. As she got into the beautiful
water she froze. I told her fear was not of God. I bound
the spirit of fear and spoke faith into her. So, in faith,
Brenda began to apply the instructions I was giving her.*

I started instructing her on how to float on her back and
then on her stomach. She was quick to do this and found
herself to be very buoyant. Even when she was on her
stomach her feet were level and on top of the water. *I
began showing Brenda different kinds of swimming strokes;
the crawl, the frog stroke, the side stroke, and many more.
And while all this instruction was going on from me, God
was personally talking to Brenda at the same time. He said*

to her, *"My hand is outstretched across the entire ocean. Are you going to trust me and let go of your fear?"* *Brenda released her fear to the Lord and she miraculously was able to pick up all the swimming instructions that I had given her with only one lesson on each stroke. Soon Brenda and I were swimming way out to the buoy.* It was the most awesome thing - she was swimming like a fish. In fact, she was swimming beyond my capabilities and skills. She was swimming like she'd swam all her life.

After we got back to the shore, she and her husband Bailey went out to swim together. Bailey was very protective of Brenda at first thinking she would need help; however, he soon found she was a great swimmer and from then on, they experienced such joyful fun together. It was as if they were falling in love all over again. Bailey was a great swimmer and had never had a companion to join him in this sport. Now he had a true friend, his wife. He was so excited - just like a kid who received his first bike at Christmas. There was a definite healing in their relationship. Both Bailey and Brenda gave God all the credit for this awesome miracle. To God be the glory, thank you Jesus! Thank you, mighty Holy Spirit.

Miracle #3
Just before departing from Montego Bay, Monette's (Jeannie's daughter) *cell phone went missing.* Everyone was coming unglued. Our transportation was coming in 15 minutes to pick us up and take us back to the ship. *I made everyone join hands and I prayed in faith that God would have the angels get that phone back on the ship somehow. God gave me the faith to believe for this and it happened.* Monette cried and cried. Benny was trying to console her, and I was hanging on in faith. Jason (an adopted family member) locked all her phones so that no one could steal her credit card information if her phone was not found.

We got back to the ship and Jason was able to get a signal that the iPhone was aboard the ship. It was found in Noah's (Monette's son) *backpack.* No one had put it there - certainly it was an angel that intervened. *Everyone knew an angel had put it there.* Many lessons were learned, and God got all the glory. *Monette totally enjoyed the rest of the trip understanding the goodness of the Lord and the power of His Word when one has faith and believes.*

Day 6
Noah's Impartation
I received from the Holy Spirit that I was to release to Noah the gifts that God had placed within me. Noah was completely willing to receive from the Lord through me. The Holy Spirit showed me what to release into Noah. I got to release from I Timothy - II Timothy, taking the 7th verse of every chapter and praying it over Noah. It was awesome how it read. I was also to impart **Ephesians 3:20** into him.

"Now unto Him that is able to do exceeding abundantly above all that we ask or think, according to the power that worketh in us."[1] (KJV)

These instructions from the Lord were also given to Noah:
- Read the story of Moses crossing over to the Promise land.
- Read Psalms 71
- Read Psalms 91
- Read the book of Revelation which is the testimony of Jesus Christ

I was told by the Holy Spirit to place my hands, which acted as the hands of Jesus Christ, upon Noah. Two things immediately came to mind: that Noah would receive wealth to pour into the kingdom of God and that he could be trusted to channel this money into God's Kingdom for God's purposes.

I then received knowledge from the Holy Spirit that Noah would be in the marketing field, that he would be a businessman having God's strategies.

When I shared this impartation with Noah's mother, Monette, she said this was a confirmation of a word given to Noah by a very seasoned prophet.

I praise God for these miracles. Noah was so receiving of this impartation and the prayer the Holy Spirit spoke over him through my vessel.

God, you get all the glory. You are so awesome. We love you so.

God speaks through the Cruise Maid Supervisor
While packing my suitcase, I could not find my prayer pictures. These are the pictures of everyone that I lay my hands on and pray over each morning. Additionally, our room safe had locked up and I was unable to open it. *I called housekeeping and they came right up and unlocked the safe. I said to the cruise maid attendant who came up to help me that I was missing my prayer pictures. She immediately responded, "Why don't you release your angels to find them." Well I did this and almost immediately the missing pictures were found.* Indeed, my angels once again came to my aid. To God be all the glory!

Summary of Cruise Miracles
Truly Lord, you lifted every member of this family to another level. They now know warfare and how to use the Word of God to fight the enemy. They know that fear is not from God, that it only opens a door for the enemy to

bring torment into their soul. ***Fear is a weapon of deception from the enemy - faith in God's Word is the only way to fight it.***

> *"Submit yourselves then to God. Resist the devil, and he will flee from you."* [2] (NIV)

> "Then I heard a triumphant voice in heaven proclaiming: "Now salvation and power are set in place, and the Kingdom reign of our God and the ruling authority of His Anointed One are established. For the accuser of our brothers and sisters who relentlessly accused them day and night before our God, has now been defeated - cast out once and for all!" [3] (TPT)

> *"They conquered him completely through the blood of the Lamb and the powerful word of His testimony. They triumphed because they did not love and cling to their own lives, even when faced with death."*[4](TPT)

You can defeat the enemy every time when you know your purpose and destiny in God. You were placed on this Earth to accomplish a mission for God. Way down inside you, He has placed within you your purpose and your calling. You just need to seek Him for it. When you find this purpose and walk in God's faith; in all humility and servanthood, walking in the truth of His Word and His commandments, the enemy cannot touch you. However, your words must be words of life and not death. Your spoken words, your imagination, your feelings and your emotions all must be submitted to God.

Jesus paid the price by shedding His blood for our sins on Calvary. He has set all free who receive Him as their Lord and Savior and are obedient to His commandments. When we accept Jesus into our hearts as our Lord and Savior, we exchange the tainted blood we received from the first Adam (who fell from God's glory and grace) and in its place, we receive the pure blood of the second Adam, Jesus Christ, who triumphed over the devil and set us free. The untainted blood of Jesus Christ makes our spirit man perfect as He is perfect. When Jesus took our sins upon the Cross of Calvary, it enabled God to see us sinless through His blood. God does not see our sins anymore. Jesus has washed away all of our sins and Father God once more can look upon His children through the blood of Jesus and see us white as snow.

How can we begin to thank you Lord for all you have done for us? Jeannie and I will continue to hold everyone up in prayer and praise God for the victory in all their lives.

God went on to reveal his grace through the miracle wedding of my nephew Howard Powell and his lovely wife, Beverley Powell. The anointing of the Holy Spirit fell upon the crowd of people and they witnessed God's goodness through the presence of the anointing of the Holy Spirit.

Miracle Wedding

Howard Alva Powell, III and Beverley Ann Marcum were married on St. Patrick's Day, March 17, 2018. They had met on St. Patrick's Day in 2017 and married one year later the next St. Patrick's Day. This date is prophetic in their divine calling for God.

Their marriage was appointed by God.

During the ceremony, the Holy Spirit fell upon the Word spoken through their ceremonial vows. It was as if a canopy of love was placed over the congregation and people wept.

This special couple asked me to marry them. I had never performed a marriage ceremony before, so I prayed on this request. They wanted a family member who knew the Lord to marry them. As I am very close to Howie (nickname), who is my nephew, I wanted to seek God's will on this matter. I had met Howie's fiancé, Beverley, one time and liked her a lot. *As I sought God concerning this marriage, He showed me that this was a divine appointment and that I was to marry them. I asked God to help me and He directed me on how to write their ceremonial vows.*

As I spent time with God concerning their vows, I was directed to read several books along with the Living Bible.

One of those books was *How to Make Your Marriage Exciting.* [5]

I did the research and the Holy Spirit wrote the ceremony.

Below is a portion of Howard and Beverley's Wedding Ceremony. It is all based on God's Word.

CEREMONY
We are gathered together here in the sight of God, and in the face of family and friends to join in holy matrimony Howard Alva Powell, III and Beverley Ann Marcum. *This is a divine union brought together by God. For God has looked upon this couple, He has seen their hearts and He has cleansed their souls and brought them both through their fiery trials to be joined together for His Kingdom purposes.*

Take note of the shamrock which is used as a symbol for St. Patrick's Day. The legend goes that the shamrock symbolizes the Holy Trinity, the three persons in God. It is joined to a stem, having three leaves on the clover. St. Patrick is noted as a patron saint and national apostle of Ireland, credited with bringing Christianity to Ireland. The trials and sufferings he endured in his life made him the humble-minded man that he became. God anointed him with might and power, and he went through the land bringing revival and reformation to Ireland.

It is no coincidence that Howard and Beverley met each other on this holy day and have chosen to marry on this day also. It is symbolic of the calling of God that is upon their lives.

WHAT IS LOVE?
[I Corinthians 13:4 through 13:6, (LB), paraphrased]
"Love is very patient and kind, never jealous or envious, never boastful or proud; never haughty or selfish or rude, Love does not demand its own way. It is not irritable or touchy. It does not hold grudges and will hardly even notice when others do it wrong. It is never glad about injustice but rejoices whenever truth wins out."

If you love someone, you will be loyal to them no matter what the cost. You will always expect the best of them, and always stand your ground in defending them. Love requires the ability to trust each other and to listen intently to what the other is speaking.

Words:
Watch the words of your mouth. They create. What you speak and what you imagine are creative forces. They create life or death. Therefore, guard your words. As you were created in God's image, you have that power to

create your world. When you control your tongue and your imagination, you control your life and your destiny. For what you speak is what you create.

Only through walking in the spirit can you maintain victory in your life. Make sure your thoughts are pure and not evil. The law of life in Christ Jesus has set us free from the law of sin and death.

For a happy marriage, you must be open and honest with each other. You must speak life to your relationship, and you will receive life. [5]

- *Be honest* - have open communication walking in truth.
- *Be loving, patient, courteous, considerate, and loyal to each another.*
- *Be forgiving*, walk in harmony together.
- *Be understanding, open and receptive to each other. Be excited about each other.*
- *Be one* - becoming one in the journey of life means that you can lift your partner up when he/she is facing a crisis or a bad day. (When one is down, the other is up. God has made you one spiritual being.)
- *Be married - sex is a gift from God.* It brings supreme intimacy.

On this special day, this union will be sealed in heaven. The union that God has ordained will become a living, life-giving entity in covenant with a living God.

Howard and little Beverley shared their personal testimonies of love for each other and why they knew God was joining them together on this holy St. Patrick's Day, March 17, 2018.

At this point there were tears in their eyes as well as stars of love. Howie presented Little Bev with a beautiful diamond ring, and Little Bev presented Howie with a Harley Davidson tire wedding ring. This brought laughter from the audience since most knew Howie's love for his Harley Davidson motorcycle. The love that flowed between these two at that moment was so sweet and precious.

For as much as Howard and Beverley have consented together in holy wedlock, and have witnessed the same before God and their family and friends, and hereto have given and pledged their love to each other, and have declared the same by giving and receiving rings, and by joining hands, I now pronounce them officially joined together for the glory of God, that they are now man and wife, in the name of the Father, and of the Son, and of the Holy Ghost.

May the Lord bless and keep you both and make His face to shine upon you and be gracious unto you. May the Lord lift up His countenance upon you and give you peace through Jesus Christ your Lord and Savior. AMEN!

I now anoint you both in the name of the Father, the Son, and the Holy Spirit to go forth into your destiny together for the glory of God.

Facing family, friends and significant others, I repeated the following: "May I present to you all, Mr. and Mrs. Howard Alva Powell, III, better known as "Howie and Little Bev.""

End Notes:
1. Ephesians 3:20 KJV
2. James 4:7 NIV

3. Revelation 12:10 TPT
4. Revelation 12:11 TPT
5. Hunter, Charles & Frances, *How to Make Your Marriage Exciting*, Hunter Books, 1972

CHAPTER 7
WEAPONS OF WARFARE - LEARNING THE LANGUAGE OF THE HOLY SPIRIT

Satan targets your weaknesses
We all have weaknesses in our soul realm. What must happen is that we must realize those weaknesses and safeguard them. As previously mentioned, there is safety in the multitude of counselors. There is much wisdom released in the counsel of God's Godly advisors directing you from the truth of the Word of God through the leading of the Holy Spirit.

"For although we live in the natural realm, we don't wage a military campaign employing human weapons, using manipulation to achieve our aims. Instead, our spiritual weapons are energized with divine power to effectively dismantle the defenses behind which people hide."[1] (TPT)
"We can demolish every deceptive fantasy that opposes God and break through every arrogant attitude that is raised up in defiance of the true knowledge of God. We capture, like prisoners of war, every thought and insist that it bow in obedience to the Anointed One." [2] (TPT)

GRACE:
Daily ask God for His grace and receive His grace. His grace enables you to walk out your destiny in Him. It gives you unmerited favor and faith to overcome all obstacles.

CLOTHE YOURSELF WITH:
Compassion, kindness, humility, gentleness and patience – and walk in love.

"Therefore, as God's chosen people, holy and dearly loved, clothe yourselves with compassion, kindness, humility, gentleness and patience." [3] (NIV)
"Bear with each other and forgive one another if any of you has a grievance against someone. Forgive as the Lord forgave you." [4] (NIV)
"And over all these virtues put on love, which binds them all together in perfect unity." [5] (NIV)

Intercession should be made daily for:
   Your country
   Your President
   Your Pastor and church body
   Your family and friends
   Intercession appointments given to you by God

Listed below are weapons that God has given us from His Word to protect ourselves, our nation, our families, our friends, and our loved ones.

PUT ON THE MIND OF CHRIST
Put on the armor of light, humility, servanthood, love, and the mind of Christ, **[I Corinthians 2:16** (KJV, paraphrased)]

PUT ON THE ARMOR OF GOD:

The armor of God consists of:
- *The belt of truth*
- *The breastplate of righteousness*
- *Placing upon your feet God's peace and rest*
- *Placing God's shield of faith in your hand*
- *Placing the helmet of salvation on your head*

Below is a more detailed explanation of God's weapons:
- *Gird your loins with truth;* Jesus Christ is the truth, the way, and the life.
- *Place the breastplate of righteousness upon yourself;* you are the righteousness of God in Christ Jesus.
- *Place upon your feet the gospel of peace,* and decree and declare that you walk in God's peace and rest.
- *Place the shield of faith (God's faith)* within your heart. It quenches every fiery dart the enemy throws at you.
- *Place on your head the helmet of salvation* which protects your mind from all thoughts thrown at you by the enemy.
- *When you take the sword of the Spirit, which is the Word of God, and dip it in the blood of the Lamb (Jesus' blood), lighting it with the torch of the Holy Spirit, you tear down Satan's evil strongholds.*

*Quoting **Galatians 2:20** (NIV) reinforces your faith.*
*"I have been crucified with Christ; it is no longer I who
live, but Christ lives in me; and the life which I now live in
the flesh I live by faith in the Son of God, who loved me and
gave Himself for me."[6]*

- It is possible through the gift of visions that the Holy Spirit will provide specific targets for you to fight in your warfare.

We use the armor of God to protect ourselves from the enemy's demonic forces and his subtle deceptions. That is why it is important to stay in the Word of God meditating daily upon it.

In *The Armor of God* - **Ephesians 6:10-18,** David Walters' Children's Bible Study book, [7]
David states the armor is given to us, but we must put it on every day. It is the armor that is mighty, rather than you who wear it. Learn to sleep with your armor on also.

*The bible says to put on the whole armor of God that you
may be able to stand against the wiles of the devil. It says
we wrestle not against flesh and blood, but against
principalities, against powers, against the rulers of the
darkness of this world, against spiritual wickedness in high
places. [**Ephesians 6:11-12**, (KJV, paraphrased.)]*

*Note: As you walk in the love and commandments of God
found in the bible, you are clothed automatically in the
armor of God. The devil then knows who you are in God,
and you become a target. He then pursues you to destroy
your destiny in God. Look at Jesus – He was first baptized
in the Jordan River, filled with the Spirit of God, and then*

went into the wilderness for 40 days. When he came out, all demonic forces knew who he was, the Son of God.

After you spend quiet, quality time with God; as you press into His presence through the Holy Spirit, He will place in your heart a knowing of your destiny - why He placed you on this Earth at this time and hour. You become aware that you are called to be a soul winner, to share the truth of Jesus Christ with the lost so that they will have eternal life in the kingdom of heaven and be spared from hell.

PUT ON THE BLOOD OF JESUS
Place (or plead) on yourself daily the blood of Jesus. *Satan cannot penetrate the blood of Jesus when you stand believing in the power of His Blood. Jesus has already won the battle for us.*
> "In Him we have redemption through His blood, the forgiveness of sins, according to the riches of His grace."[8] (KJV)

Having done all of the above, place your thoughts, your words, your feelings, and your emotions under the Word of God. *Speak life and not death. For the words that you sow will surely grow a crop.* That is how Satan deceives.

Satan uses human beings to speak condemnation and words of death and harm concerning themselves and others. In this way, he creates a life of misery for you and others. *You create your own life through your words.* Now my mouth says nothing contrary to what the Word of God says. *When you grasp this concept of who you are and what your destiny in Christ is, the devil cannot touch you when you stand in faith believing God's word.*
> "For in Him we live and move and have our being. As some of your own poets have said, we are His offspring." [9] (NIV)

"Who has known the mind of the Lord so as to instruct him. But we have the mind of Christ." [10] (NIV)

RECITE PSALMS 91 OVER YOURSELF
Make sure you personalize it – making it your own.
Verses 1-16
> *"Whoever dwells in the shelter of the Most High will rest in the shadow of the Almighty."* [11] (NIV)
> *"I will say of the Lord, "He is my refuge and my fortress, my God, in whom I trust."* [12] (NIV)

This is an end-time Psalm. We are living in the end times and God is releasing to us His mighty weapons of warfare. This is one of them. Use it with authority.

PLACING THE NO TRESPASSING SIGN ON YOUR PROPERTY, AS WELL AS BUILDINGS OF GOVERNANCE. (This also includes your church)
This is a prayer God's intercessors can use if desired.

Surround these dwellings with God's angels. Frame a mental picture in your mind of angels holding up a sign that reads: 'No Trespassing Satan'. This property belongs to the Lord Jesus Christ. Then cover the outside ground, within the boundary lines, with the blood of Jesus.

Then, go inside the dwellings and permeate the atmosphere with the blood of Jesus after which you place God's angels in the four corners of every room. Visualize these angels singing praises unto Jesus.

Recently I have learned that Satanists place demonic spirits under our dwellings. So, I have started applying the blood of Jesus under our homes, businesses, and governmental buildings. To do this, use the sword of the spirit (God's word) covered with the blood of Jesus and lit by the torch of the Holy Spirit.

OTHER SUGGESTIONS:
- *Playing Christian anointed music in your home wards off evil spirits.*
- *When playing the Word of God in your home demons and evil spirits flee.*

Satan comes in through the eye of your soul. So, I would caution you to watch what you allow your eyes to view. We must keep our vessels clean and holy. For God has instructed us to be holy as He is holy.

"But now He has reconciled you by Christ's physical body through death to present you holy in His sight, without blemish and free from accusations."[13] (NIV)

In other words, Christ has made us holy through the shedding of His blood on Calvary. He who the Son sets free is free indeed - and His blood has set us free.

"It is for freedom that Christ has set us free. Stand firm, then, and do not let yourselves be burdened again by a yoke of slavery."[14] (NIV)

IN HIM
"Let me be clear, the Anointed One has set us free - not partially, but completely and wonderfully free! We must always cherish this truth and stubbornly refuse to go back into the bondage of our past."

From Kenneth E. Hagin Sr.'s pamphlet entitled "IN HIM" He states on page 10:
As you read some of the "in Christ", "in Him", "in Whom", etc. scriptures, they won't seem real to you.

It may not seem as though you really have what these scriptures say you have in Him. But, if you will begin to confess with your mouth, because you do believe God's Word in your heart saying: "This is mine. This is who I am. This is what I have." Then it will become reality to you. It is already real in the spirit realm. But we want it to become real in this physical realm - the Earth atmosphere where we live in our flesh.[15]

It is always with the heart that man believes - and with his mouth he makes his confession. When you believe a thing in your heart and confess it with your mouth - then it becomes real to you. *Faith's confessions create realities.* **Romans 10:10.**

"For with the heart one believes unto righteousness, and with the mouth confession is made unto salvation."[16] (NKJV)

Learning the language of the Holy Spirit:
Often the Holy Spirit speaks through the Word of God. It becomes illuminated - like a beam of light flowing out of the Word into your heart. *This is called the rhema word of God. It is alive, it is living.* Although you may have read the Word many times before, when it's a rhema word it will jump off the pages of the bible into your heart and become personal to you. You will know what that word means and how it applies to your life. Then it is up to you to activate what the Holy Spirit is telling you to do (No matter how the Holy Spirit speaks, it will always agree with the Word).

He speaks through visions and pictures in your imagination.
You are to test these visions to make sure they are from God. They must line up with the Word of God. They must flow in love, kindness, righteousness and peace.

All imaginings (pictures that appear in your mind) that are contrary to the Word of God, *that divide, and harm people, are from the opposite side – darkness and gloom. These are from the demonic realm. You must cast these thoughts away in the Name of Jesus and they will go. The bible tells us that we are to submit ourselves to God, resist the devil and he will flee from us (James 4:7).* You have the authority and power to do this when you have accepted Jesus as your Lord and Savior.

God speaks to you by divine appointment - such as bringing to your attention a matter that is quickened or made alive in your spirit. He will confirm this to you through different sources, usually there will be three confirmations. After you receive these confirmations, be obedient to activate His directives.

God can place a knowing in your spirit: you just know when something is going to happen, or you just know it will happen. You must make sure that word follows the truth of the scriptures found in the bible. Then after you have done this, you just stand on that word and praise God for His mercies and for the unveiling of that word to manifest on the Earth.

God can speak to you through billboards, or headlines in media sources. There is something on the billboard or media headline that will just grab your spirit. Then He will continue to confirm that word [through other means] and bring it to pass. Again, everything must be in line with His commandments and His Holy Word.

He can speak through prayer with like-minded Christians. He can show you visions and confirm His plans and purposes to you. You then call His plans and purposes forth into the Earth and they manifest for the glory of God.

"Meditate the picture God gives you, imagine and picture it. Align your mind with God's pictures."[17]

If you have been called into heavy intercession, here are a few more suggestions you may want to add to the above list:

Communion:

When taking communion, you are remembering your covenant with God through Jesus and all Jesus did for you. You are humbly coming before God in repentance of any and all sins, known or unknown. The blood of Jesus washes away all your sins according to **1 John 1:9**. When you are born again, you become the righteousness of God in Christ. It is the blood of Jesus that cleanses you of all your sins. Father God sees you then as white as snow through the blood of Jesus. As a believer, if you sin and then repent of your sin, all unrighteousness is washed away by the blood of Jesus. Communion is a powerful reminder of the sacrifice that Jesus paid for your redemption.

Taking the Holy Sacraments:
*This consists of unleavened bread and wine or juice taken to symbolize the body and the blood sacrifice that Jesus paid for our sins on the Cross of Calvary. He was our sin offering. (**Luke 22:19-20**)*

Jesus took the bread, gave thanks and broke it, and gave it to his disciples saying, "This is My body which is given for you; do this in remembrance of Me." [18] (NKJV)
"Likewise, He also took the cup after supper saying, "This cup is the new covenant in My blood, which is shed for you"[19] (NKJV)

Commander of the Morning Prayer

You can find this prayer on the internet. There are several versions. I say this prayer before I go to bed at night. In the prayer you decree that Satan cannot steal your destiny based on God's Word.

RECAP

Before you leave your house in the morning make sure to cover yourself as outlined above. *Placing on yourself, your nation and its leaders, and your family, friends and loved ones:*

- *The Blood of Jesus*
- *The Armor of God*
- *Psalms 91*

End Notes:

1. 2 Corinthians 10:3-4 TPT
2. 2 Corinthians 10:5 TPT
3. Colossians 3:12 NIV
4. Colossians 3:13 NIV
5. Colossians 3:14 NIV
6. Galatians 2:20 NIV
7. Walters, David, *The Armor of God Ephesians 6:10-18*, Good News Fellowship Ministries, 2015
8. Ephesians 1:7 KJV
9. Acts. 17:28 NIV
10. I Corinthians 2:16 NIV
11. Psalms 91:1 NIV
12. Psalms 91:2 NIV
13. Colossians 1:22 NIV
14. Galatians 5:1 NIV
15. Hagin, Kenneth E, *IN HIM*, Kenneth Hagin Ministries, Inc., 1975
16. Romans 10:10 NKJV
17. Virkler, Mark, *4 Keys to Hearing the Word of God*, Destiny Image Publisher, Inc., 2010
18. Luke 22:19 NKJV
19. Luke 22:20 NKJV

JETTA NASTALLY

INTO THE ARMS OF JESUS

CHAPTER 8
SATAN DECEIVES THROUGH WITCHCRAFT

A little-known secret of the enemy, that few are cognizant of, is that once people go under witchcraft, they lose all of their identify. They no longer know who they are in Christ, they only know they are saved. They are no longer a threat to the devil. They no longer have the vision of winning souls for the kingdom of God.

We all need to be keenly aware of the ploys and tactics of the enemy. He enters our minds through openings that we create through our words, imaginations, emotions and feelings. When we fall into his traps, these openings draw us out of the commandments of the Lord into our carnal nature. Just like Eve fell into the sin of pride, the devil comes in subtly to deceive and destroy.

Satan finds a crack (a loophole) in your soul realm and engages your mind to corrupt God's Word and make you think it is wrong.

A few of these openings include:
- *doubts*
- *unbelief*
- *fears*
- *temptations*
- *anger*
- *unholy speech*
- *impure thoughts*
- *pride*
- *selfishness*
- *compromising the Word of God*

*You must know that God has forgiven all of your sins.
When you accept Christ into your heart, you have no past.*

Satan is a liar and a thief.
*"The thief comes only to steal and kill and destroy; I
have come that they may have life and have it to the
full."[1] (NIV)*

*God says in His Word: "If you love Me you will keep My
commandments." When you do this, He protects you from
all the wiles of the devil and you walk in His peace. His
angels accompany you everywhere.* It is such a blessing to
be a child of God walking in His love, being obedient to
His Word.
*"If you keep My commands, you will remain in My
love, just as I have kept My Father's commands and
remain in His love."[2] (NIV)*
"For He will command His angels concerning you to
guard you in all your ways."[3] (NIV)

*It's our responsibility to make sure there are no openings
that the enemy can enter in through.* Watch your words.
Surely, he is looking for those areas and weaknesses in our
lives to attack us and take us away from our divine destiny
for God's Kingdom.

*Let us all walk in the Lord's grace: Asking God each day
for His grace and receiving it each day in Jesus name
AMEN.* What is grace? Grace is unmerited favor. It is
simply listening to the voice of the Holy Spirit and
activating what He tells us to do. It is walking in the truth
that He imparts to your spirit. It sets us free from the ploys
of the enemy. *Grace is walking in humility and
servanthood before the Lord.*

There may be challenging times when you feel you simply cannot love another, or you simply cannot be obedient to God's Word. At times like that you can simply say, "Holy Spirit I give this to you. I am unable to do this. Please activate Your grace for me in this situation." And He will do it. All you need to do is turn it over to Him. For example, you may have an eating disorder. You may not have the will power in your flesh to control your eating (that chocolate cake looks so good). *All you need to do is say, "Holy Spirit give me the will power to resist this temptation." Turn it over to Him, and He will give you His grace for the situation.* As a believer you already have self-control as one of the fruits of the Spirit listed in **Galatians 5:22-23**. We tap into these fruits through grace. If you are serious with God and need help, the Holy Spirit is your Helper.

Satan deceives with intent to destroy your God-given destiny through deception
"In the beginning God created the heavens and the Earth."[4] (NIV)

There are three forces in the Earth. (Three voices you can hear in your head)
- *The Spirit of God*
- *The Spirit of man*
- *The Spirit of Satan*

We were made to control the atmosphere around us.
We must receive our words that we speak by revelation of the Holy Spirit. You cannot name it and claim it. That becomes self-willed and it is not inspired by God but by flesh."[5]

THE SPIRIT OF GOD

It is simple to distinguish which voice you are hearing. *The Spirit of God is always filled with peace, love, gentleness, and kindness. It reflects the image of God. God is love.* His words will always line up with the written Word of God.

> *"But the fruit of the Spirit is love, joy, peace, forbearance, kindness, goodness, faithfulness"*[6] (NIV) … "gentleness and self-control. Against such things there is no law."[7] (NIV)

This is how you can tell when a thought is from either the Holy Spirit or from Satan - thoughts of God are righteous and good, thoughts from Satan are evil and destructive. If they are from God, you must put them into action. If they are from Satan, you must counteract them with the Word of God.

If you have been a person of procrastination, you will have to be trained by the Holy Spirit to activate immediately what He is telling you to do. *God is training us to respond to His instructions quickly.* This can easily save your life in the future. Let us say you were traveling down a road and a picture or message comes across your mind. It could even be the word 'STOP' or 'PULL OVER'. When you are obedient, you perhaps spared yourself from an accident - possibly caused by someone running a red light. It is important to learn to listen and understand the language of the Holy Spirit. He protects you from life and death situations.

THE SPIRIT OF MAN

The Spirit of man - when man is redeemed and walking in the spirit, his spirit voice which is his conscience can also be trusted. Man's conscience then is a safe guide. For the Word tells us:

"Therefore, if anyone is in Christ, the new creation has come; The old has gone, the new is here!"[8] (NIV)

THE SPIRIT OF SATAN
The bible says that Satan is a thief and he comes to rob and to steal.

"The thief comes only to steal and kill and destroy; I have come that they may have life and have it to the full."[9] (NIV)

Everything that is contrary to the Word of God: Hatred, bitterness, revenge, unforgiveness - all these come from the enemy's side. The enemy can put pictures in your mind just like the Holy Spirit does. But you can spot his pictures very quickly because they are founded upon evil intents.

When these thoughts are evil you reject them - cast them away from your mind and put in its place what the Word says. For instance, if the thought is to hate, then you immediately place love into your mind and heart. If you are unable to love this person that comes before you, then give it to the Holy Spirit, and ask Him to love through you. It really does work. God is amazing.

Satan has no creative abilities. He is not omnipresent as God is. He is not everywhere at one time. He uses his demonic angels and demons to do his dirty work. This means the only way he can touch you is through: the words of your mouth, your imagination, your feelings, and your emotions. If you speak negative about yourself, that empowers him to put the words that you spoke into action.

If you cannot speak what you feel, you can instead say: "I have such and such symptoms, but the Word says I am healed, and I am going to stand on the Word until I see the manifestation of my healing."

> "But it was because of our rebellious deeds that he was pierced and because of our sins that he was crushed. He endured the punishment that made us completely whole, and in His wounding, we found our healing."[10] (TPT)
> "Like wayward sheep, we have all wandered astray. Each of us has turned from God's paths and chosen our own way, even so Yahweh laid the guilt of our every sin upon Him."[11] (TPT)
>
> "He Himself bore our sins in His body on the cross, so that we might die to sins and live for righteousness; by His wounds you have been healed."[12] (NIV)

The Holy Spirit will bring us into peace as we continually praise the Lord for His goodness and place our soul and body under the power of the Holy Spirit. We then ask Him for His grace, and we receive His grace every day so that we can walk joyfully before our Lord in complete victory.

Satan sends up smoke screens. Everything he does is a deception to lure you into his web of destruction which ultimately brings you into his world of ugliness, despair, brokenness and hopelessness. We can prevent this from happening by following God's Word and walking in the light of His love.

To inherit the promises of the Word, you must believe the Word and receive its truths into your heart. You must speak that Word and stand in faith until it comes to pass. *You must know who you are in Christ Jesus, and who He is in you. You must have the faith of God and know your authority* (Once born again, each believer is given a measure of God's own faith according to **Romans 12:3**). By using this God-given faith, the devil is no match for you; for he can no longer deceive you through his lies - you are anchored in God's truth. Your feet are on the rock of Jesus Christ and you stand immoveable. Yes, there is warfare, but by standing in faith you take down the enemy's strongholds every time.

> "Because through Christ Jesus the law of the Spirit who gives life has set you free from the law of sin and death."[13] (NIV)

God's redeemed can call heavenly things onto Earth in faith. **Matthew 6:10** (KJV) *"Thy kingdom come. Thy will be done on Earth, as it is in heaven."* *However, these things must be given to them by the Holy Spirit who receives His instructions from Father God.* And when these spirit-led visions, dreams, or words are spoken into the atmosphere, there is a spiritual shift that occurs. The presence of God's light comes forth to break through the darkness of the enemy. It removes the devil's deceptions from the eyes of the blinded. They see who Jesus is and the price He paid to grant them entrance into heaven. Heaven is a place of love where there is no more pain - only joy, laughter and love.

> "The Spirit of the Sovereign Lord is on Me, because the Lord has anointed Me to proclaim good news to the poor. He has sent Me to bind up the brokenhearted, to proclaim freedom for the captives and release from darkness the prisoners,"[14] (NIV)

END NOTES:
1. John 10:10 NIV
2. John 15:10 NIV
3. Psalms 91:11 NIV
4. Genesis 1:1 NIV

5. Johnson, Neville, *The Power of Words*, Satellite Productions, 2008 (DVD)
6. Galatians 5:22 NIV
7. Galatians 5:23 NIV
8. 2 Corinthians 5:17 NIV
9. John 10:10 NIV
10. Isaiah 53:5 TPT
11. Isaiah 53:6 TPT
12. I Peter 2:24 NIV
13. Romans 8:2 NIV
14. Isaiah 61:1 NIV

CHAPTER 9
SCAMMED ONCE, SCAMMED TWICE

Satan will always try to keep you from obtaining God's blessings and from fulfilling your destiny. He will enter in through some void in your life. This is exactly what happened to me.

Scamming has become a billion-dollar business. Listed below are a few examples and statistics of this insidious practice:

From 2004 to 2017, $11 billion were paid in penalties by pharmaceutical companies for unlawful promotions which included promotion for off-label drug benefits (Reported by Kvia.com).

AARP Bulletin Publication, October 2019, Vol. 60, No. 'A' issue:
Sweepstakes scams stage a comeback. It has been reported by the Federal Trade Commission that $713.3 million dollars was lost to fraud in the First Half of 2019. These Impostors seek cash in advance of a 'prize'.

Kvia.com:
Online romance scammers are busy stealing money and hearts across the United States. The Federal Trade Commission has warned that scams that prey on vulnerable people cost Americans more money than any other fraud reported to the agency last year. It was reported that online romance scammers conned more than 21,000 people into sending more than $143 million in such scams in 2018 alone.

The top 10 scams of 2019:

1) *Investment scams*
2) *Dating & romance*
3) *False billing*
4) *Hacking*
5) *Remote access scams*
6) *Online shopping scams*
7) *Threat to Life, arrest or other*
8) *Identity theft*
9) *Classified scams*
10) *Pyramid schemes*

I hope that through sharing my experience with others, that they can benefit and become aware of the many traps one can fall prey to. I am going to recap my experiences being scammed to give you an idea how these scam artists operate.

Unfortunately, scamming has become a big business - raping others of their hard-earned money through deception and fraudulent activities. These people are constantly looking for targets. They use media such as Facebook to find you. They can also find your telephone number and if you do not answer, they will often leave a message. Through listening to that message, it can pull you into thinking what they are saying is truth. After establishing a connection with you, they will redirect you onto a site where they can woo you with their demonic potions.

As I mentioned previously, the first time I was scammed (conned), it was through a void in desiring to be loved by a man after my husband James' Earthly death.

This scam happened through the internet when a man claiming to be a general in the army contacted me through

Facebook. He immediately led me out of Facebook to another site. Foolishly, I downloaded a program he asked me to put onto my computer.

This man said he was stationed somewhere in Africa on a UN peace keeping mission. He proceeded to send me love notes, romantic music and songs that filled a void in me to be loved by a man.

At the time I was corresponding with this man portraying himself as an army general, I was also praying and ministering to a close female friend located on the US East Coast. We had been praying together for almost three years (three times a day) for her deliverance from the spirit of witchcraft. Her parents were heavily involved in deep witchcraft and upon her birth they had offered her up to Satan. Her sisters had surrendered their lives to Satan because of the fierce warfare against them when they tried to embrace truth. I was way over my head on this assignment in trying to help her with a mixture of spirit and flesh.

In trying to appease the general and my friend between their two different time zones, I went ten days with practically no sleep. Well, that does not work. God does not bless foolishness.

After having fallen for all this love stuff, I was requested to send money to fly this man to Texas so that we could marry. I was initially directed to send money through Walmart. However, since the money requested was a large sum, Walmart would not allow that amount of money to be released as it could be a potential scam. I wouldn't listen as I was certain this was the real deal.

Well it was a scam, and I fell for it so completely. No one was able to convince me otherwise. I was so delusional that I believed it all to be fact, as the desires of my flesh were very strong in wanting to be loved by a man.

As Walmart would not allow the money to be wired, I was then told to wire money from my bank account where I was able to send the money. In the end, my retirement 401K account was completely drained. When my son came to my rescue, all my financial accounts had been compromised and had to be cancelled and new accounts opened.

After my recovery, I thought I had learned the lessons I needed to learn and would never fall prey to another scam. However, two years later I was scammed again, but this time it was not due to a void in my life, but due to poor judgement.

This second scam featured a person impersonating an Apple employee - they even had an Apple logo that appeared on my cell phone screen. They stated they were from the Apple Recovery Department for fraud.

These people are experts at twisting the truth and spinning a lie into something that seems real. In order to confirm to me that they were telling the truth, I allowed them to have access to my desktop computer. They pulled up some report that indicated my User ID had been compromised and that my name was being used to promote sex trafficking for small children. I was horrified. They said they could fix this problem, but it would cost me $500 initially, but that all monies would be refunded after the problem was resolved. They then directed me to purchase a Game Stop Card at a specific Kroger's grocery store. They did not want me to hang the phone up, even when I went into the store to purchase the card. They also mentioned not to tell the clerk to whom the card would be given. Warning: never fall for this scam!

After I purchased the card, they wanted me to give them the number on the card, and then scratch off the code number on the back. It turns out that this is the pin number that they need to get their money. This scam artist then told me that there were three layers to this problem and that I would need to get another $500 for them to make these corrections. Foolish me, I went back and got another card and gave them the numbers. He then told me the card did not work and to go back for another. Yes, I went back for another. He reported that card did not work as well. I told him I was out of money and that was it. Well he wanted me to borrow the money. Now at that point my mind became coherent and I started to sense that something was not right.

When I returned home, I called Apple and they told me that it was a scam. Apple said they would never notify customers of such things via a text or a phone call.

I then called the Houston, Harris County police, and they sent an officer to review my case. He was at my door within 15 minutes after I had called. The officer said that there is no way to trace these scam artists. He said they go into the App store online and purchase numbers that cannot be traced. He said that because I willingly went and purchased the card, that it could not be reported as fraud. When you willingly give your money, it is no longer a fraudulent case. Cards such as this cannot be traced. When the thieves receive your money from this cash card, your money is gone forever into their hands. *My suggestion to everyone is that if a message is left on your cell phone, do not answer it unless it is a person that you know and they are in your phone directory.*

Because I used a card that is untraceable, the scam artist never received my personal information like Social Security number, bank account numbers, and driver's license information. This meant that all I needed to do to keep them from accessing my bank accounts (because I had let him into my HP desktop computer), was to change my password to my banking account in my desktop computer. I did this immediately.

I would like to add that these people have no feelings for you. This is the way they make a living and their hearts are as cold as stone. If you were bleeding in the street and the buzzards were picking at your body, it would not bother their conscience one bit. They are evil people; cold, calloused and used by the devil to rape people who are vulnerable. Only a mind depraved of righteousness would take another human being and use them for their evil pleasures and their financial gain.

When I contacted my son and my sister about what had happened, they asked why I had not called them. So, I spent some time with the Lord and asked Him how this could happen to me since I walk in truth and am guided by the Holy Spirit. This is what the Lord said to me: "First, you did not stop to ask me, if this is a yes or a no (true or false)." God went on to say, "I would have told you had you asked Me. Second, you broke one of My commandments. On the seventh day of creation I ended My work and rested. I blessed the seventh day and sanctified it and called it a day of rest."

I had been going without adequate sleep for over three months, 3-5 hours per night of sleep with one nap of approximately 30 minutes in the afternoon. I had pushed myself into exhaustion. Since I am a person with a manic personality, always up and joyful, I cannot rationalize, nor use any common sense to navigate in truth when I am exhausted.

To remedy this problem, I was instructed to take one day a week and REST. So, now I take one full day and spend it reading, praying, and seeking an intimate relationship with Father God, the Lord Jesus Christ and the mighty Holy Spirit.

May we all stay within the protection of God's commandments and words and seek God for His wisdom and direction in all that we do and say. To embrace total victory on Earth, you must walk by the spirit of God within you, following the commandments of God's holy Word.

In today's world there is such a fight against truth. We blatantly see good being called evil, and evil being called good. God never created man to hate one another and use and abuse one another.

Truly LOVE is the answer to all because God is love; therefore, let us love our brethren and pray for those who are deceived and do wicked works abusing and using others for their own selfish gain. All of us have a choice. God is love, joy, peace and righteousness. Walking with Him daily, through the guidance of the Holy Spirit, brings unspeakable joy.

kvia.com offers these additional tips to avoid being scammed:

Things to pay attention to with internet dating

- Do not be led off Facebook or other official sites to another web carrier
- Do not fall in love too quickly
- Do not send money without face-to-face contact

Phone Scams

Scam artists are now impersonating charitable outreaches for known celebrities. The Federal Trade Commission says if you unexpectedly hear from a big name for a charitable donation check it out:

1) Slow down. Before you send money, talk with someone you trust.
2) Do some research. Search online for the celebrity's name plus "scam". Never send money, gift cards or prepaid debit cards to anyone you have not met-including famous people.
3) Report your experience to the Federal Trade Commission.
4) Stop and ask yourself the question: Why is this star I have never met calling me?

CHAPTER 10
MY REQUEST TO GOD -
THE DESIRE OF MY HEART

*Lord your Word, your truth (Jesus), is what changes people. For **John 1:1** says "In the beginning was the Word, and the Word was with God, and the Word was God. Jesus is the Word.*

*My journey started with Dick Mills' Ministry 47 years ago, when he prophesied **Psalms 30:5** to me.*

(Note: Dick Mills had a supernatural gift imparted to him by God. He was taken to heaven and God downloaded His Word, chapter and verse, from Genesis to Revelation into his being. He then would minister the Word through scripture, as directed by the Holy Spirit). I too believe God will impart unto me the download of His Word in its entirety.

> *"For His anger endureth but a moment, in His favour is life: weeping may endure for a night but joy cometh in the morning."*[1] (KJV)

Under this anointing and word, my journey with God began. I have never forgotten that Word, "weeping shall endure for the night, but joy will come in the morning". The manifestation of this word took many years to come forth - over 47 years. My weeping did endure for many years as my dream died. It was only later that it would be resurrected in God's perfect time.

I was also given that same year, by an established prophet of God, the scripture from [***Ezekiel 36:26-27 (KJV, paraphrased)]*** where God said, *"...I will remove your* *stony heart and give you a heart of flesh - My heart of love."*

The Lord has now placed me on the mountain top looking down at Satan and his cohorts. I am taking my authority, in the spirit, over the enemy's strongholds, in Christ Jesus in heaven places. I receive and believe You Lord for this anointing. You have given me confirmations in the spirit that enable me to stand on this awesome desire of my heart. You have looked upon my heart and found it washed and cleansed by the blood of Jesus. You have tried me and taken the broken pieces and put them together for Your glory. *It is only You God who can put us together, through weaving Your love throughout our hearts, so that we are able to fulfill our destiny on Earth for You.*

I am overjoyed that You never gave up on me. I am filled with gratitude that you have imparted your faith into my heart to lead many souls into the kingdom of God. Each day I draw closer and closer to You, to hear your heartbeat, to stand in intercession for Your people. I can think of no greater blessing than that which You have extended to me.

Thank You Lord God Almighty, You are so faithful, so loving and so kind. To God be the glory for the things You have done!

"One Minute with God"[2]
- I pray that people will have a divine one-minute encounter with God that turns their hearts to truth, and they surrender ALL to JESUS.
- *God, I thank you that in a single moment You can change lives, giving eternal life to all who seek You and receive Jesus as their savior. You can bring Your truth, Your love, and Your glory unto all who surrender their lives unto You.* We are carriers of

Your glory and it is imparted through us to change
the atmosphere around us so that others are
changed and set free from the bondages found in
this world.

*Let the words of our mouths be edifying and not
condemning of others. Let us steward the gifts You have
given unto us correctly in love. This applies to our
brothers and sisters in Christ as well as to the lost. Let us
walk in humility and servanthood. Let our flesh be put
under our Spirit. Let us be alive unto God.*
Thank you, God, that You never give up on us. Your
patience is everlasting. Your mercies and grace are
extended to us throughout eternity. Let us walk in praise
and thanksgiving to You realizing these blessings. We are
blessed to be a blessing to others. *Help us Holy Spirit to
walk with You in the Love of God. Perfect us so that Your
divine destiny will come to pass in our lives for the Glory of
God.*

Daily Decrees for Accessing Abundance - Discover the Power of Job 22 by Joshua Fowler[3]

*Through reciting these daily decrees each day for over
a year, they became rhema to my spirit. There are 22
decrees. Studies show that it takes 21 days to change a
mindset. Within these 21 days, God took me to another
level in the Spirit. By decreeing and declaring His
Word, I was changed.* Below are listed the scriptures
decreed each day:

DAY:

1. **THE DECISION DECREE:** Job 22:8 (AMPC)
   "You shall also decide and decree a thing, and it
   shall be established for you; and the light [of God's
   favor] shall shine upon your ways."

121

2. **THE BLESSING DECREE:** Ephesians 1:3 (NKJV) "Blessed be the God and Father of our Lord Jesus Christ, who has blessed us with every spiritual blessing in the heavenly places in Christ."

3. **THE ABUNDANCE DECREE:** 2 Corinthians 9:8 (NKJV) "And God is able to make all grace abound toward you, that you, always having all sufficiency in all things, may have an abundance for every good work.

4. *THE ROYAL DECREE:* I Peter 2:9 (NKJV) *"But you are a chosen generation, a royal priesthood, a holy nation, His own special people, that you may proclaim the praises of Him who called you out of darkness into His marvelous light."*

5. **THE DREAMERS DECREE:** Joel 2:28 (NKJV) "And it shall come to pass afterward that I will pour out My Spirit on all flesh; your sons and your daughters shall prophesy, your old men shall dream dreams, your young men shall see visions."

6. **THE HARVEST OF SOULS:** Matthew 9:37 (NKJV) Then (Jesus) said to His disciples, "The harvest truly is plentiful, but the laborers are few."

7. **THE FAVOR DECREE:** Luke 2:52 (NKJV) "And Jesus increased in wisdom and stature, and in favor with God and men." **Psalms 5:12** (NKJV) "For You, O Lord, will bless the righteous; with favor You will surround Him as with a shield."

8. **THE POWER DECREE:** Deuteronomy 8:18 (NKJV) "And you shall remember the Lord your God, for it is He who gives you power to get wealth, that He may establish His covenant which He swore to your fathers, as it is this day."

9. **THE TIMING DECREE**: **Ecclesiastes 3:1-2**
(NKJV) "To everything there is a season, a time for every purpose under heaven: a time to be born, and a time to die; a time to plant, and a time to pluck what is planted."

10. **THE DOUBLE DECREE:** **Isaiah 61:7** (NKJV)
"Instead of your shame you shall have double honor, and instead of confusion they shall rejoice in their portion. Therefore, they shall possess double; everlasting joy shall be theirs."

11. ***THE DOERS DECREE:*** **James *1:22* *(NKJV)***
"But be doers of the Word, and not hearers only, deceiving yourselves."

12. **THE GOVERNOR'S DECREE:** **Zechariah 12:6**
(NKJV) "In that day I will make the governors of Judah like a firepan in the woodpile, and like a fiery torch in the sheaves; they shall devour all the surrounding peoples on the right hand and on the left, but Jerusalem shall be inhabited again in her own place - Jerusalem."

13. **THE HEIR'S DECREE:** **Romans 8:16-17**
(NKJV) "The Spirit Himself bears witness with our spirit that we are children of God, and if children, then heirs - heirs of God and joint heirs with Christ, if indeed we suffer with Him that we may also be gloried together."

14. **THE INCREASE DECREE:** **I Corinthians 3:7**
(NKJV) "So neither he who plants is anything, nor he who waters, but God who gives the increase." **Psalms 115:14** (NIV) "May the Lord cause you to flourish, both you and your children." **Isaiah 9:7** (NKJV) "Of the increase of His government and peace there will be no end, upon the throne of David and over His Kingdom, to order it and

establish it with judgment and justice from that time forward, even forever. The zeal of the Lord of hosts will perform this."

15. ***THE PROSPERITY DECREE:*** **Job 8:7** (NKJV) *"Though your beginning was small, yet your latter end would increase abundantly."*

16. **THE SOWERS DECREE:** **2 Corinthians 9:10** (NKJV) "Now may He who supplies seed to the sower, and bread for food, supply and multiply the seed you have sown and increase the fruits of your righteousness," …

17. **THE REAPERS DECREE:** **Luke 6:38** (NKJV) "Give, and it will be given to you: good measure, pressed down, shaken together, and running over will be put into your bosom. For with the same measure that you use, it will be measured back to you."

18. **THE EXPANSION DECREE:** **Isaiah 54:1-6** (MSG) "Sing, barren woman, who has never had a baby. Fill the air with song, you who've never experienced childbirth! You're ending up with far more children than all those childbearing women" God says so! "Clear lots of ground for your tents! Make your tents large. Spread out! Think big! Use plenty of rope, drive the tent pegs deep. You're going to need lots of elbow room for your growing family. You're going to take over whole nations; you're going to resettle abandoned cities. Don't be afraid - you're not going to be embarrassed. Don't hold back - you're not going to come up short. You'll forget all about the humiliations of your youth, and the indignities of being a widow will fade from memory. For your Maker is your bridegroom, His name, God of the Angel Armies!

Your Redeemer is The Holy of Israel, known as God of the whole Earth."

19. *THE DEBT FREE DECREE:* **Deuteronomy 28: 12-13** (NKJV) *"The Lord will open to you His good treasure, the heavens, to give the rain to your land in its season,* and to bless all the work of your hand. You shall lend to many nations, but you shall not borrow. **:13** And the Lord will make you the head and not the tail; you shall be above only, and not be beneath, if you heed the commandments of the Lord your God, which I command you today, and are careful to observe them." **Romans 13:8** (NKJV) *"Owe no one anything except to love one another, for he who loves another has fulfilled the law."* **Psalms 34:10** (NKJV) *"The young lions lack and suffer hunger; but those who seek the Lord shall not lack any good thing."*

20. *THE FIRE DECREE:* **Hebrews 12:29** (NKJV) *"For our God is a consuming fire.* **2 Timothy 1:6-7** (NJKV) "Therefore I remind you to stir up the gift of God which is in you through the laying on of my hands. :7 For God has not given us a spirit of fear, but of power and of love and of a sound mind."

21. *THE ACCELERATION DECREE:* **Ezekiel 12:28** (NKJV) Therefore say to them, *"Thus says the Lord God: 'None of My Words will be postponed any more,* but the Word which I speak will be done,' says the Lord God." **Jeremiah 1:12** (NKJV) "Then the Lord said to me, 'You have seen well, for I am ready to perform My Word.'"

22. **THE SUPER DECREE:** **Ephesians 3:20-21** (NKJV) "Now to Him who is able to do exceedingly abundantly above all that we ask or think, according to the power that works in us, **:21**

to Him be glory in the church by Christ Jesus to all generations, forever and ever. Amen.

23. **<u>NAME YOUR PERSONAL DECREE:</u>** Find a scripture and decree and declare it over yourself daily.

Below are words from a song sung by the late Kelley Varner. These words touched my heart, as indeed, *we do have to walk in faith trusting God to perform His Word.* For we overcome through the blood of the Lamb and the word of our testimony.

"ALL IS WELL"[4]

"All is well no matter what my eyes may see,
All is well no matter what my ears might hear.
I know that all is well because My God will fight for me."
(God fights for me when I walk in faith
believing His Word.)

End Notes:
1. Psalms 30:5 KJV
2. Dr. Ellis, Keith, *One Minute with God,* It's Supernatural & Messianic Vision, Inc., 2015
3. Fowler, Joshua, *Daily Decrees for Accessing Abundance: Discover the Power of Job 22,* Whitaker House, 2017
4. Varner, Kelley, CD "Treasures - New and Old, Praise Tabernacle,

INTRODUCTION TO "GOD SPEAKS" SECTION

After I received Jesus as My Lord and Savior, He placed within my heart a knowing of my calling. I ran from it for years because He likened me to the prophet in I Kings who disobeyed God's commandments and was eaten by a lion after being deceived by a fallen prophet. This prophet was not to eat nor drink until he returned home, but *he listened to another prophet's voice and disobeyed God's instructions - for that disobedience he was killed by a lion on his return home.*

> **1 Kings 13:24** (KJV): "And when he was gone, a lion met him by the way, and slew him: and his carcass was cast in the way, and the ass stood by it, the lion also stood by the carcass."

I wanted no part of that ministry, and so for almost 47 years of my life I ran from my calling. What God was trying to say to me was that I needed to be on a vertical with Him, meaning I needed to learn to listen to His voice through the person of the Holy Spirit and follow what He told me to do. Well, we have a very patient God. For he waited for almost 47 years for me to come to the end of Jetta. He let me go through all my many trials until I surrendered all unto Him. Truly, I no longer want to live by my soul by using my intellect and my reasoning.

I say all that to introduce this section of GOD SPEAKS.
*God has gifted me with the ability to sit at the computer
and listen to God's voice and type that which He tells
me. So, although this section is written through my
vessel, it is God speaking to His people through me. He
is very serious about all of you reaching your destiny.*
God paid a great price by releasing His Son to come to
Earth and be crucified for our sins so that we could
once again be His family. And Jesus, in obedience,
carried out the plans of the Father. We too must
surrender all to finish our destiny and bring in the lost
so that they will not spend eternity in the damnation of
hell. Jesus died to set ALL free - only through His
blood can mankind be saved. There is no other way.

I do hope that you will take to heart what God has
written to you in this section of GOD SPEAKS. It is all
Word related and written in a personal way so that you
can understand how much God really loves you and
wants you to come into His family of love.

*May God's grace and mercy take you to your God
ordained destiny in Christ Jesus.* For Jesus has indeed
paid the price for your sins, you need only to embrace
Him as your savior and move on to complete your
destiny on Earth for Him. Holy Spirit I ask that you
shower your anointing, your creative glory upon the
words of this book. I ask that you open the truth to all
the hearts of the lost and to the many saved who are not
walking in accordance to your Word.

CHAPTER 11
GOD SPEAKS:

MEDITATE ON THE FULLNESS OF THE MEASURE OF THE STATURE OF CHRIST

Look up, look up into the heavens. Can you not see the immense vastness of My creation? You see in part - not in whole. For the fullness of the stature of Christ is indeed immeasurable. You cannot conceive with your mind's eye the fullness of My love for you.

I sent My Son Jesus Christ to redeem you back to me from the enemy who deceived Eve by enticing her into his trap of lies. She began to conceive in her mind thoughts that I was withholding something from her. It was then that the sin of pride entered her. This is the same sin that entered Satan and caused him to fall from My grace. He was able to deceive a third of the angels in heaven to follow him. They left their home in heaven of light and glory to become Satan's cohorts of evil and destruction.

I speak to you directly - do not fall into Satan's traps. Do not fall for his lies. Wake up! Wake up My children for the hour is near where My hand of judgment will fall upon this Earth and there will be a mighty shaking that will occur. When you die, there is life after death. You must choose who you will serve before your departure from Earth. Through My goodness, I have provided you forgiveness of every sin you have ever committed. This is a gift that My Son gave to you on the Cross of Calvary to set you free. Through His blood He redeemed you, for I wanted a family that I could love and that would love Me.

For you to receive this free gift, you must embrace My Son Jesus Christ as your Savior. You must invite Him into your heart and yield your vessel up to Me in obedience to My commandments which are found in My Word [**James 1:22** (KJV, Paraphrased)]. Do not merely listen to the Word, and in so deceive yourselves. You must do what it says. Anyone who listens to the Word but does not do what it says is like someone who looks at his face in the mirror and after looking at himself goes away and immediately forgets what he looks like. But whoever looks intently into the perfect law that gives freedom and continues in it - not forgetting what they have heard but doing it - they will be blessed in what they do. This is the gateway to heaven - a place where there is no sorrow or suffering, a place so great, vast, and magnificent, that it is impossible to grasp with your Earthly mind.

The second place that is also eternal is a place of darkness and despair. Those dwelling in Satan's dominion live in torment day and night and it is eternal. *The enemy of your soul is pride.*

Hatred and all that goes with it are ploys of the enemy to rob you of My gifts of love and goodness which are received by embracing My Son Jesus as your Lord and Savior.

Come, come, children and dine at My table. It is a big table, able to hold you all and cleanse all of the filth, shame, and evil deeds that you have been entrapped in. The blood of Jesus cleanses you from all filth and sets you free.

Again, I say, you cannot conceive the fullness of the stature of Christ. It is immense and beyond Earthly mental capacities. Look up, look up! You must surrender your imagination, your feelings, your emotions, your words to me and I will fill your heart with My love. Come I say.

Come dine at My table. Release it all to Me - be a doer of My Word. *After receiving My Son as your Lord and Savior, you need then only to release yourself to the mighty Holy Spirit in you to be transformed into the image of Christ.*

The hour has come when I am shortening the time of growth in My people. When you are serious and have truly yielded your vessel to Me and are being led by the Holy Spirit and walking in the Spirit of God, you shall grow quickly. *I will use you to transform this world by praying forth My Word over My people.*

For you see children, I have placed you on Earth at this exact hour, because in heaven there are no time zones. In heaven I look down and I see all the difficulties that you will endure: all the joys, all the sadness, all the victories. I see everything.

You have a book in heaven and in it is written your Earthly destiny. So, lift your eyes up, and know that My grace and My mercies are with you. *My mercies are renewed every morning and My grace is given for you through Jesus Christ My Son. He brought grace and truth to you. Jesus is the truth, the way, and the life.*

The fiery trials you have been through are to purge you and set you free from the clutches of the evil one. Once you pass through the fire, you are cleansed and lifted up by My faith to call the supernatural miracles of the spirit into the Earthly realm so that they will come to pass. For you see, I gave authority to man when I created him. Jesus redeemed you back to Me and through His blood you have become His sons and daughters. You speak what the Holy Spirit directs you to speak using the name of Jesus and it comes to pass because it is from the Father.

Through the blood of Jesus, you are one. One in mind, one in heart, and one in purpose for winning souls for the kingdom of heaven. This is why you were created and placed on Earth at this hour. So, children seek Me with all your heart. Rise above the pain that you have experienced. Lift your eyes, there is a rainbow of promises for you to embrace.

You must release all torment and fear from your being. You must embrace love: the language of heaven. I am love and, therefore, you too must be love. You can only do this when you surrender all to Me and let the mighty Holy Spirit run your life. Your life then becomes a life of peace and rest. When you have issues that you cannot conquer in the natural realm, all you must do is surrender the problem to the Holy Spirit. Tell Him that you release your soul, your feelings, your emotions, your intellect, and your will to Him. Ask Him to take over the situation and take a step back. He is amazing. He will take that problem from you, lift it right off your shoulders, and enable you to walk in love toward that person. This is the secret of heaven. There is nothing impossible to those that love Me and serve Me and walk according to My Word and commandments.

So, children grasp this truth. Seek Me with all your heart. Surrender all your pains to Me. Accept My Son as your Savior and turn your life over to the Holy Spirit. Then, and only then, will you know the true peace, rest, and love of My person. *I am a Spirit and you must communicate with Me in spirit.* The Holy Spirit will teach you how to do this. It is an exciting journey. Each day you experience challenges, but you can overcome them all with the help of your friend the Holy Spirit.

Come children for I am waiting. All My life I have wanted a family to love and be loved by. The tests you go through on Earth cleanse your soul, so we become like-minded and can communicate with each other in the spirit realm. My love for you far surpasses your understanding.

Come, come dine at My table. I am waiting to embrace you with My unconditional love - a pure love that has only goodness, righteousness, and blessings for you to share. Come, come dine at My table. I am waiting, I am waiting - the time is short. *I draw you through My love into an eternal life of blessings.*

From your Father in heaven, God Almighty

JETTA NASTALLY

CHAPTER 12
GOD SPEAKS:

THE JOY OF THE LORD IS YOUR STRENGTH

Do you know what the joy of the Lord really is? Do you know that it is the color of yellow, the color of the SUN? *It is light; it is creative life.*

Why does My Word say it is your strength? This is because where there is joy there is no sorrow. Where there is joy there is abundance of laughter which is merriment to your soul. *Joy is a weapon against the enemy of your soul. It shuts out darkness so that despair cannot envelope you and pull you down.* Regardless of your situation, if you focus on My goodness, My light and love will flood your soul. The fact is that if you praise Me through your darkest hour, at the end of the tunnel there will be light and life and joy.

The enemy of your soul will try to pull you into a web of despair, but if you will hold onto the image of My Son redeeming you back to me on the Cross at Calvary you will be set free. He was your sin offering and through His blood you are set free from your sins. Only *through embracing Jesus as your savior will you find yourself able to go through your trials* on Earth in peace. Look up, look up! Cheer up, cheer up! For Christ has set you free from the chains and bondages that Satan has implanted in your mind. *You must change your mindset, your imagination, your words, your thoughts, and your actions to line up with My Holy Word and in so doing you will march right out of the miry muck that Satan has entangled you in through his deceptions.*

Perhaps your situation started from family abuse down through the generations. *I tell you children; the blood of Jesus Christ has broken the strongholds and chains that have bound you and your family in bondage all these years.* You have but to look up, to cheer up, and to confess with your mouth My Son as your Lord and Savior and walk in alignment with His Holy Word. When you do this a door opens in the Spirit and you can walk through this portal into a land of peace, joy, and freedom. *For He who the Son sets free is free indeed.*

You must be able, in your mind's eye, to picture and see yourself free. Use your imagination and envision this new you - see yourself free, then begin to apply all your senses to the victory of that freedom. *There is hope in your despair if you can grasp the truth of true joy. There will be no more sorrow, you will be lifted up and given My grace which is sufficient to take you through the trial of your circumstance.*

Children you will never know the depths of My love for you. I am your Father in heaven who awaits your arrival to become My family. But *you all are on Earth at this hour for a purpose. I have a destiny for you. That destiny takes you into a world of joyous victory because it brings you out of self into love for your fellow man.* It brings you into a world where giving is more blessed than receiving. Your Spirit envelops and absorbs your soul. Your Spirit is Holy and set apart for great things.

Yes, the weapon of joy is a gift of great worth. For where the light and life of joy dwells, so does the presence of the Holy Spirit. The Holy Spirit instructs you and guides you in the ways that you should go. He envelops you with My wisdom, My understanding, My counsel and might, and My revelatory knowledge. All this He bestows upon you to make you a light for My glory to bring the lost into the kingdom of heaven and to save them from the darkness and gloom and doom of the enemy's hell. This brings you into joy unspeakable; into the victorious life of an overcomer who is set free from the clutches of Satan's deception.

Having done all, stand, and see the completed salvation of the Lord. For indeed the joy of the Lord is your strength. *You are loved, you are My family. And Christ died to set you free so that you in turn could set others free by being My vessel of light and truth to the world.*

Shine out, shine out, My children of light. For indeed the joy of the Lord is your weapon of glory to dispatch the darkness around you. Go forth into that light. *Know who you are in Christ. Know your destiny in Him* and shine, shine forth to illuminate the darkness. For a candle cannot be hidden under the bed, it must be brought forth to shine and illuminate the room with the brightness of its light.

You are My light; the light of Christ is within you. *You are that candle that is set high on a hill so others can see your light.* You draw others to the light of Christ within you and break the yokes, bondages, and deceptions that the darkness and atmosphere of the world have encased them in.

Rejoice, rejoice, for the joy of the Lord has set you free to be that light on the hill for man to see.

From your Father in heaven, God Almighty.

JETTA NASTALLY

CHAPTER 13
GOD SPEAKS:

THERE IS NO CONDEMNATION IN CHRIST JESUS

Do you not know that in Christ Jesus there is no condemnation? The voice that keeps tormenting you and telling you that you are worthless is the voice of Satan. It tells you to look at your past to remember all your wrong doings. Do not listen to this voice - tune it out. Christ Jesus died on Calvary to set you free. He took all your past sins, absorbed them in His body, and gave to you in exchange His perfect character and nature. *I, your Father in heaven, look at you through the blood of Jesus and I see you as white as snow. All your sins have been washed away and all things have been made new.* You are a new creature in Christ Jesus; old things have passed away and all things have become new. So, children do not listen to any words that condemn you. I do not see your sin. *I do not condemn you nor look at your past.* As soon as you receive My Son as your Lord and Savior and walk in obedience to the Holy Spirit, then I no longer remember your sins. They are wiped away never to be remembered again.

Condemnation brings torment, and torment is based on fear and not on faith. That is how you know the voice of the enemy; he will always let you know that you are worthless, and he will always bring up your past trying to belittle you, trying to get you to swallow the pill of shame, regret, and sorrow. But look up! Look up to the cross on Calvary. *Jesus took those sins from you on that cross - never to be remembered again. He set you free from the weight of your past and you no longer need carry those burdens and sorrows.* Remember My nature is love. The words of your

139

mouth must display goodness and mercy and love towards others. There is nowhere in My Word that speaks of your sin after you have embraced Jesus as your Savior. His blood cleanses you from all your past sins and they are no more. When the enemy sneaks into your mind with condemning and tormenting thoughts of your past, do not receive them. They are contrary to My Word. You must know who you are in Christ Jesus. *My Word tells you in* **James 4:7** (KJV) *"Submit yourself to God, resist the devil and he will flee from you."* It tells you to draw near to Me and I will draw near to you. It tells you to cleanse your hands and purify your hearts. It tells you not to be double minded.

Stand in the freedom that Christ Jesus has given you and be not entangled in the yoke of bondage again. Do not go backwards. *Look! Look straight ahead. Keep your mind and thoughts on what I have for you ahead. You have a future, you have a destiny, you have a purpose. Seek Me with all your heart and I shall be found.* Seek to know Me intimately and I shall open doors for you that no man can close. I shall part your Red Sea and you shall cross over to your promised land.

Think upon things that are good, righteous, wholesome, kind and fruitful. You were created to be fruitful. For your tree to have fruit that is beneficial for growth, you must think, act, and walk with your eyes into your destiny. *Seek Me with all your heart and I will show you what your destiny is in Christ Jesus. Each of My creations have different and unique gifts* - I want you to utilize them. I want to bring you all into My glory so that you shine out to a lost world. I want to use you to impart hope to the hopeless. I want you to impart love to the lost. For this to occur, you must know who you are in Christ Jesus. Without a doubt you must realize your worth and move forward. *Your life began anew when you embraced Jesus Christ as your Savior.* Indeed, you became a new creation. Do not look back. Learn who you are in Christ Jesus and push forward to release your vessel to Me, so that I can miraculously turn you into My vessel of love to those who are lost and without hope.

Yes, there is no condemnation in Christ Jesus. He washed it all away with His pure blood. Since He was immaculately conceived by the Holy Spirit falling upon Mary, His blood is not tainted like the blood of Adam. By the overshadowing of the Holy Spirit upon Mary, Jesus was immaculately conceived. Therefore, Jesus' blood is pure and not of this Earth. Adam fell into the deception of Satan and all men after him fell into that sin. Jesus redeemed us back to the Father by His pure blood. You have lived under this heaviness here on Earth all your lives - but no more. *Through embracing Jesus as your Savior, you are freed from the clutches of the enemy. You need only to read My Word, practice My Word and walk by the instructions of the Holy Spirit within your being.* When you stand in the authority given to you by Jesus, the enemy has no power over you. Satan is not creative; he uses your words to create. He uses your mouth to vocalize negativism - *what you speak is what you get. The devil creates through your mouth, your feelings, your imagination, and your spoken words.* Remember, when you submit yourself to the authority of the Holy Spirit, and are led by Him into truth, He will teach you all things. You will quickly gain knowledge of the Spirit realm and learn how to create good things.

You were made to spread hope, love, peace, and healing to a world void of understanding. Look up! Look straight ahead into the eyes of Jesus and He shall always embrace you with His love.

I love you all so very much. Stand and proclaim your victory in Christ Jesus. Be not moved by your circumstances. *Rebuke the enemy and he will flee. Enter your promised land which is lit with the brightness of My glory.*

Remember, there is no condemnation in Christ Jesus, He has set you free.

Your Loving Father in heaven, God Almighty

CHAPTER 14
GOD SPEAKS:

MY MERCIES ENDURE FOREVER

I love My creations and want My sons and daughters to come into My glory, for in it you will experience the fullness of My love and you will walk in peace and harmony with all My creations - living plants and animals included. I love each one of you and want you to become a part of My heavenly family where there is joy unspeakable.

"My mercies and love endure forever..." In **Psalms 136:1-16**, I have outlined below the power of those mercies:

Note: "For His mercies endure forever" - this statement comes after every verse of who God is.

I am the God of gods; for My mercy endures forever
I am the Lord of lords
I alone do great wonders
By My wisdom the heavens are made
I stretched out the Earth above the waters
I made the great lights
The sun to rule by day
The moon and stars to rule by night
I smote Egypt in their firstborn
I brought out Israel from among them
With My strong hand, and with My outstretched arm
I divided the Red Sea into parts
I made Israel to pass through the midst of it
But I overthrew Pharaoh and his host in the Red Sea
I led My people through the wilderness
I smote great kings - Sihon, King of the Amorites
And Og, King of Bashan

I gave their land for an inheritance
A heritage unto Israel My servant
I remembered their low estate
I redeemed them from their enemies
I give food to all flesh
O give thanks unto Me, the God of heaven
For My mercy endures forever.

I am the Lord of creation. I created all things. I laid the foundations of the Earth when I created Earth and breathed life upon it along with the Theos (aka The Trinity: the Father, the Son, and the Holy Spirit). I created the Garden of Eden and placed Adam in that Garden to rule over all within that garden. He named all the animals. There was such unity and love between man, plants and animals; but when Adam was deceived by Satan and disobeyed Me and ate of the forbidden tree of knowledge, he lost his spiritual covering. The heaviness of that sin of disobedience fell upon My heart for I knew the road ahead for mankind would be very hard and that many would fall from My ways and be deceived into gross darkness.

But all was not lost, for I was to redeem mankind back to Myself through the blood of My Son, Jesus Christ. He willingly gave His life to take human form and be the sacrifice for your sins. He was impregnated into Mary by the breath of the Holy Spirit and she immaculately conceived. Since the blood of mankind had been tainted, it could not be used to redeem mankind back to Me.

From the very hour that Jesus was born, warfare from Satan came forth. Herod wanted Jesus killed. When the wisemen sought information regarding the birth of the King of Kings, Herod deceptively said he would come and honor this King too. But this was not true. For in his mind's eye there was no king except himself. The shepherds in the fields brought a staff for the King, they were alerted to His birth by the angels who appeared in the sky. The wisemen were warned in a dream not to go back to King Herod, but to return by another route. They were guided by a star to Jesus. They brought gifts to Him of gold, frankincense, and myrrh.

It was through this miracle of Christ's birth that My mercies were poured out upon this Earth for man once again to know truth, to know righteousness, and to become My family.

So, children, come to My table and dine and let us become one: one in heart, one in mind, and one in purpose. *You were created to be free; to love, laugh and walk in truth and righteousness. When you embrace My Son, Jesus Christ, as your savior, you are freed of all the sins that you have committed on this Earth.* His blood cleanses you from all unrighteousness and you become the righteousness of God in Christ Jesus. You receive the sinless nature of Christ and I look upon you and see nothing but the pure blood of Jesus that covers you and makes your sins white as snow – your sins are remembered no more.

You were created to bless each other - to share Jesus with a world that is without hope. You need only to embrace Him as your Savior and walk in the light of His Word by the Holy Spirit and you indeed will become a new creature. You will fulfill your destiny - reaching out to others and sharing the truth with them so that they can, in turn, be set free.

I love you children. I invite you to come dine at My table with me. There is room for you all.

Your Loving Father in heaven, God Almighty.

JETTA NASTALLY

CHAPTER 15
GOD SPEAKS:

MY GRACE IS SUFFICIENT

Without My grace, you are powerless to achieve your destiny on Earth. My grace is the impartation from the Holy Spirit to walk in the light of My love, My peace, My righteousness, and My purpose for your life. It raises you into another dimension. It enables you to walk by the Spirit of God; to listen and to act upon the words that I place in your mind and heart.

Many have said that grace is a cup of My unmerited favor towards you. Yes, *you did not earn grace, Jesus earned it for you through the shedding of His precious blood on Calvary for your sins.* Grace is a gift of My love and the love of Christ for you. When you embrace grace and walk in the light of My love, My favor is extended to you. Grace is also an impartation of My miraculous supernatural hand of healing and restoration unto you.

Fret not about the situations that you encounter in life. You need only to surrender all unto Jesus and confess Him as your Lord and Savior, and His redemptive blood will set you free from the yoke of bondage that the enemy has entrapped you in. After embracing Jesus as your Savior, there shall be no more despair, no more darkness, no more hopelessness. You have only to grasp this precious gift of My grace to walk in the peace and love that My Son bestowed upon you on the Cross of Calvary.

Think it not strange that you encounter fiery trials in your life, for the enemy has cloaked you with his coat of deception so that you cannot see My light. Look up and connect with Me in the spirit realm, for Christ has redeemed you from the curse of the law and has set you free. [**Romans 8:1-4** (KJV, paraphrased)] tells you that the law of the Spirit of Life in Christ Jesus has set you free from the law of sin and death. So now the case is closed. There remains no accusing voice of condemnation against those who are joined in life-union with Jesus, the Anointed One. For the law of the Spirit of Life flowing through the anointing of Jesus has liberated you from the law of sin and death. For I, Father God, achieved through My Son what the law was unable to accomplish, for the law was limited by the weakness of human nature. I sent My Son in human form to you to identify with your human weaknesses. My Son gave His body to be the sin offering for you. His blood erases all your sins and sets you free from all bondages. Now every righteous requirement of the law can be fulfilled through the Anointed One living His life in you. And you are free to live, not according to your flesh, but by the dynamic power of the Holy Spirit within you!

For you to be set free, you must turn and change the perspective of your mind. You must see yourself set free. You must proclaim My Word over yourself and your mind will soon be renewed to know who you are in Christ Jesus. You must think on good things. Your imagination must have thoughts of living life. You must activate love in your life. You must embrace My righteousness and walk in the light of it. You say, how can I do this? I will tell you that the only way you can do this is by surrendering your life to Jesus and being led by the mighty Holy Spirit within you.

For you to be led of the Spirit within you, you must be a student of the Word. The Word is truth and you must walk in it. Ask Me to give you a hunger for My Word. Reach up and grab that gift. I shall give it to you. There is nothing that I cannot do for you if you will trust Me and obey My commandments. They are not grievous or difficult when you walk by the Spirit of God within you.

Come dine at My table. There is room for you all. There is nothing I cannot do for you when you ask Me in faith, believing My Word, and knowing who you are in My Son. *He conquered the world of evil on the cross. All that you need is already supplied for you on Earth. You need only to trust and believe.*

Call upon Me and I will answer. I will speak to you in dreams and in visions. Come away and spend time with Me. Do not let the electronics of this day consume all your time. Do not be persuaded by false media and news reports. Focus on good and not evil. Come and spend time alone with Me. Walk and talk with Me in My garden of love. I shall teach you through the Holy Spirit the language of love and I shall impart to you the gift of My grace. I will impart the ability for you to rise above the turmoil and ploys of the enemy. I will take you out of the darkness into My brilliant light. *There is no darkness in Me. I shall shine upon your darkness with My light and you shall see how glorious My love is for thee.*

Today can be the first day of your life. For when you embrace Jesus Christ as your Savior, you are born again. Old things pass away, and all things become new. No longer do you have chains on your feet, nor are you handcuffed. You are no longer a prisoner; you have been given your freedom as a new man or woman in the Lord Jesus Christ. You then must embrace your new identity and stand in what the Word tells you that you are in Christ Jesus. Then you can change into that new creation that I have ordained you to be.

Yes, then you can be My vessel to reach the lost and share My love with a world in darkness. I am waiting to embrace you with My love. *You are My beloved and I am yours. My goodness is renewed every morning and My grace is sufficient for your every need.*

I love you, Your Father in heaven, God Almighty.

CHAPTER 16
GOD SPEAKS

VANITY, VANITY, ALL IS VANITY

"Vanity, vanity all is vanity", were the words that King Solomon wrote in Ecclesiastes. I tell you children this statement is true when you live outside of My Word. King Solomon was given the gift of wisdom. He had great riches; He lacked for nothing. He withheld no joy from himself. *He sought women from far off countries who worshipped other gods. He allowed those women to bring their gods into his land and to place their idols on the hills. He eventually forsook Me and served other gods. At the end of King Solomon's life, he repented and made it into heaven for My mercy endures forever.*

One cannot in the end expect to be blessed when they live in the life of the world around them that has foreign gods for their idols.

I bless My people who are true and faithful to Me - who honor Me with their lips and with their actions. I tell you children, there is nothing I won't do for My children who are faithful and true to My commandments listed in My Holy Word. All you need to do is accept My Son as your Lord and Savior and serve Him in faithfulness and truth. You do this by embracing My Word and walking in faith:

Hebrews 11:1 (TPT)
"Now faith brings our hopes into reality and becomes the foundation needed to acquire the things we long for: It is all the evidence required to prove what is still unseen. "

Having done all, stand through the fiery trials and temptations that Satan brings before you. He is a master deceiver; do not listen to the negative voices he sends your way. When you cross over the mountain of tribulations and receive your prize, you will be lifted to another realm. You will be lifted into heavenly places to see the atmosphere below. You will be flying high like an eagle above your circumstances.

Then, and only then, will you be able to lift others up out of their hopelessness into the light of My glory. This is what it is all about. I am the eternal God of all creation. I had no beginning and I have no ending. Your Spirit lives on forever. You have the choice to live in heaven or to live in hell. Riches and wealth shall pass away, but My love never ceases. The kingdom of God is not a matter of rules; the kingdom of God is the heavenly realm of divine love. It is filled with My love, righteousness, peace, and joy.

There is no new thing under the sun. That which has been done is that which shall be done. Life is a cycle. You live now in the last days. You were chosen to be My representatives on this Earth to bring in the lost. Take your stand, and having done all, stand and see the salvation of the Lord.

Revelations 3:20: (TPT)
"Behold, I'm standing at the door knocking. If your heart is open to hear My voice, and you open the door within, I will come into you and feast with you, and you will feast with me."

I will give you the keys that open the door of your destiny, and as you activate the instructions given to you from the Holy Spirit, you will learn quickly each step to take. You will experience life more abundantly.

So, open the door of your heart and let Me come in and feast with you. Live a life of victory and not a life of hopelessness. I love you all more than you will ever know. *Provision has been made for you to enjoy the freedom of heaven and the blessings that rest therein.* Just come, come drink of the wine of the Spirit of God. Be refreshed, be encouraged, and be lifted high into the glory of My presence.

I love you, Your Father in heaven, God Almighty

JETTA NASTALLY

CHAPTER 17
GOD SPEAKS:

HAVE THE FAITH OF GOD - FAITH IS MEASURABLE

My children, there are three dimensions of faith:

Little Faith - **Matthew 8:26; Luke 12:28**
This faith relies on everything and everybody except God.
It is faith in the world system - belief only in what the
physical eye can see. It is filled with pride and blocks all
Godly truth.

Great Faith - **Matthew 8:10; Matthew 8:5-13; Matthew 9: 20-22)**
*You will see this in My Word demonstrated by the centurion
who believed Jesus could heal without going to his home to
lay hands on his servant. For, you see, he was a man of
authority.* When Jesus spoke the word to him, He believed
it to transpire immediately. Jesus commended him for this
great faith. His servant was healed without Jesus traveling
to his home. Jesus said to him, "I have not found such
great faith in all of Israel."

Then there was the woman with an issue of blood. She
pressed through the crowd to touch the hem of Jesus'
garment and virtue went out from Jesus into her body
healing her blood condition of 18 years.

*I tell you children; you all can receive great faith as you
move out from the darkness that encompasses you and
press into the healing light of Jesus Christ My Son.*

You have only to believe in the free gift that My Son, Jesus
Christ, bought for you on the Cross of Calvary. *Embrace*

Him as your Savior and Lord and He will impart to you His gift of eternal life:

> *"He (God) has made Him to be sin for us, who knew no sin; that we might be made the righteousness of God in Him."* **2 Corinthians 5:21** (KJV).

There was no other way to redeem mankind back to Me, your Father in heaven, who loves you so. The first Adam sold mankind out to the devil; therefore, redemption could only come through untainted blood. Christ was that sacrifice to redeem you back to Me. He was the second Adam, the Adam of the Spirit of Life.

[**1 Corinthians 15:45** (NIV, paraphrased)] "...The first man Adam became a living being; the last Adam, a life-giving spirit." The first Adam was made a living soul, the second Adam (Jesus) was made a quickening spirit. The first Adam was Earthly, and last Adam (Jesus) was heavenly.

The law made nothing perfect, but Jesus was made a priest forever after the order of Melchizedek.
1   "For this Melchizedek, king of Salem, priest of the Most High God, who met Abraham returning from the slaughter of the kings and blessed him,
2   To whom also Abraham gave a tenth part of all, first being translated "king of righteousness," and then also king of Salem meaning, "king of peace,"
3   This king of Salem was without father, without mother, without genealogy, having neither beginning of days nor end of life, but was made like the Son of God and remains a priest continually (forever)." [**Hebrews 7:1-3** (NKJV, paraphrased)]

Jesus came through the tribe of Judah; and made you priests and kings after the order of Melchizedek.

5 "So also Christ did not glorify Himself to become the High Priest, but it was He who said to Him:
"You are my Son, today I have begotten You.". 6 As He also says in another place: "You are a priest forever according to the order of Melchizedek."
[**Hebrews 5:5-6** (NKJV, paraphrased)]

Melchizedek was the king of Salem, who was My priest – the priest of the Most High God.
19 And he blessed him and said: "Blessed be Abram of God Most High, Possessor of heaven and earth;
20 And blessed be God Most High, who has delivered your enemies into your hand. And he gave him a tithe of all."
[**Genesis 14:18-23** (NKJV, paraphrased)].

"But ye are a chosen generation, a royal priesthood, an holy nation, a peculiar people; that ye should shew forth the praises of Him who hath called you out of darkness into His marvelous light." **I Peter 2:9** (KJV)

Jesus has no beginning and no ending. He has made you priests and kings after the order of Melchizedek. After *Jesus* was crucified, He descended into hell and *took the keys of sin and death from Satan and then He arose to sit at My right hand in heaven where He makes intercession for all My children day and night. He loves you all so.*

When you embrace Jesus as your Lord and Savior, you are given the mind of Christ [**I Corinthians 2:16** (KJV, paraphrased)]. *However, you must put your soul, and your flesh (your body and your carnal way of thinking) under your spirit in order to embrace the mind of Christ.* This is a process. You then become like minded with Jesus Christ, having one purpose and one heart. *We have three persons within us (the Father, the Son, and the Holy Spirit).* Just as your fingers have three parts and operate as one, so it is with the Godhead.

- *I am your Father God - Of whom the whole family in heaven and Earth is named*
- *Jesus, the Son, is the redeemer of mankind*
- *The Holy Spirit broods over creation to bring the Shekinah glory cloud upon the Earth. This brings forth My glory and presence which dissipates all darkness that surrounds you.*

Perfect Faith
Perfect faith is when your faith enables you to always overcome every obstacle. It has eyes to see the future, to imagine that future and call it forth.

Hebrews 11:3 (TPT)
"Faith empowers us to see that the universe was created and beautifully coordinated by the power of My words! I your Father in heaven spoke and the invisible realm gave birth to all that is seen."

Hebrews 11:1 (TPT)
"Now faith brings our hopes into reality and becomes the foundation needed to acquire the things we long for. It is all the evidence required to prove what is still unseen."

Perfect faith sees what I, Father God, want you to call into existence on Earth today and then speaks it forth in faith.

My Kingdom realm can be manifested on Earth through you speaking it forth as you are instructed by the Holy Spirit. This causes My plans and purposes to be fulfilled on Earth as it is in heaven.

I need My children of faith to call My will on Earth into existence: that is what "Perfect Faith" is all about – bringing light to the darkness on the Earth. Remember, all things are possible with me, your Father in heaven, when you walk in faith and believe.

So, rejoice, for your redemption comes forth with might and power. *My love shall break the shackles of hell and darkness from your soul and you will be lifted up to see the Person of Truth, the redeemer of all mankind.*

Come, My children – lift your eyes and see the illumination of My glory. For My light is lifted high unto My holy hill to be seen by all. All darkness shall dissipate, and My glory shall come forth to set the captives free.

I love you, Your Father in heaven, God Almighty

JETTA NASTALLY

CHAPTER 18
GOD SPEAKS:

THOUGH YOU WALK THROUGH THE VALLEY OF THE SHADOW OF DEATH, YOU WILL FEAR NO EVIL FOR MY ROD & STAFF THEY COMFORT YOU.

Children do not doubt My love for you. Jesus, My Son the good shepherd, has redeemed you back to me with His blood on Calvary. Accept this gift of redemption and be free.

John 10:1-3 (TPT)
Jesus said to the Pharisees, "Listen to this eternal truth: The person who sneaks over the wall to enter into the sheep pen, rather than coming through the gate, reveals himself as a thief coming to steal. But the true Shepherd walks right up to the gate, and because the gatekeeper knows who he is, he opens the gate to let him in. And the sheep recognize the voice of the true Shepherd, for He calls His own by name and leads them out, for they belong to Him."

[John 10:11 (TPT, paraphrased)]
"Jesus is the Good Shepherd who laid down His life as a sacrifice for the sheep." (You are my sheep.)

You are the sheep that Jesus has redeemed back to Me. I am your Father in whom the whole family in heaven and Earth is named. I am the Great "I Am". With the sacrificial redemptive blood of My Son, Jesus Christ, every circumstance, sin, burden, problem, guilt, fear, shame, hurt, and rejection that you have experienced on Earth has been erased by the blood of Jesus.

You have only to embrace this gift and walk and be led by the mighty Holy Spirit which Jesus imparts unto you when you accept Him as your Savior.

I have said in My Word in the Old Testament:

Isaiah 43:1 (TPT)
"Listen, Jacob, to the One who created you, Israel, to the one who shaped who you are. Do not fear, for I, your Kinsman-Redeemer, will rescue you. I have called you by name, and you are mine."

Mary Magdalene wept when she went to the tomb of Jesus and found it empty. However, Jesus so loved her that He stopped by to comfort her on His way back to heaven after He had taken the keys of sin and death from Satan. He first ascended into hell and took those keys from Satan which released you from Satan's entrapments.

[John 20:15-16 (KJV, paraphrased)].
Mary did not recognize Jesus until he called her by name, and then she immediately said, "… Raboni" which means teacher.

John 10:27 (KJV)
"My sheep listen to My Voice, I know them, and they follow Me."

Before the foundation of the Earth was formed, your name was written in your book in heaven. The greatest gift you will ever experience is the gift of salvation through the redemptive blood of My Son, Jesus Christ.

You can walk through that shadow of death victorious through accepting My Son's sacrifice for you. Accept Him into your heart this day by faith. My Word says in

Hebrews 11:1 (KJV) "NOW faith is the substance of things hoped for, the evidence of things not seen."

By faith we understand that the worlds were framed by the Word of God; so that the things which are seen were not made of things which do appear. **Hebrews 11:3** (KJV)

You ask me, "How can I walk through the shadow of death and fear no evil?" Again, I say, *fear is a weapon of the devil to torment you. Perfect love has no fear; and I am perfect love. All that I do is in love. Even the trials and fires that you go through, I turn them around, so that you will one day embrace truth - My Son Jesus Christ as your Savior. Then and only then will you come into peace and rest in me.*

So, I say children, come dine at My table where there is room for everyone who embraces My Son as their Lord and Savior. This requires turning your life over completely to the Holy Spirit. You will receive the Holy Spirit, the Comforter, after you have received Jesus as your savior.

I will instruct you and guide you (through the person of the Holy Spirit) in the way you should go; The Holy Spirit will lead you forth with My eyes as your guide. [**Psalms 32:8** (NKJV, paraphrased)]

The Word that goes forth out of my mouth; It shall not return to me void, but it shall accomplish that which I please, and it shall prosper in the thing for which I sent it. [**Isaiah 55:11** (KJV, paraphrased)]

For My thoughts are not your thoughts, neither are your ways My ways; for as the heavens are higher than the Earth, so are My ways higher than your ways, and My thoughts higher than your thoughts. [**Isaiah 55: 8-9** (KJV, paraphrased)]

When you speak forth the pure Word that the Holy Spirit gives you to proclaim on Earth, you then activate My will to come to pass on Earth.

Embrace My gift of love, and you will always walk in My peace and rest. Come, come dine at My table of love.

I love you, Your Father in heaven, God Almighty

CHAPTER 19
GOD SPEAKS:

THE LOVE OF GOD

Children, to understand love you must start to function in it. In this world that you now dwell in, Satan has the legal dominion over Earth's domain. The first Adam gave that to him when he disobeyed Me in the Garden of Eden. The second Adam (Jesus Christ) made provision for your redemption through His blood - thus bringing you back to Me and the family of God where there is love, peace, rest, and joy unspeakable. However, for you to utilize this gift of redemption, you must surrender all to Me by embracing My Son, Jesus Christ, as your Lord and Savior. It is then that the gift of the Holy Spirit is released unto you, and when you surrender all to Him, and follow His instructions which are from Me, your Father in heaven, then your life becomes one of love and peace.

1 Corinthians 13 tells you what love is. There is no way that you can walk in love, without surrendering your life completely to the Lord Jesus Christ. For it is through the blood of Jesus that I can look upon you and see you white as snow without sin. *Love suffers long and is kind, it does not envy.*

I Corinthians 13: 1-9, 11-13 (TPT)
1. If I were to speak with eloquence in Earth's many languages, and in the heavenly tongues of angels, yet I didn't express myself with love, my words would be reduced to the hollow sound of nothing more than a clanging cymbal.
2. And if I were to have the gift of prophecy with a profound understanding of God's hidden secrets, and if I possessed unending supernatural knowledge, and if I had

the greatest gift of faith that could move mountains, but have never learned to love, then I am nothing.

3. And if I were to be so generous as to give away everything I owned to feed the poor, and to offer my body to be burned as a martyr, without the pure motive of love, I would gain nothing of value.

4. Love is large and incredibly patient. Love is gentle and consistently kind to all. It refuses to be jealous when blessings come to others. Love does not brag about one's achievements nor inflate its own importance.

5. *Love does not traffic in shame and selfishly seek its own honor.* Love is not easily irritated or quick to take offense.

6. Love joyfully celebrates honesty and finds no delight in what is wrong.

7. Love is a safe place of shelter, for it never stops believing the best for others.

8. *Love never takes failure as defeat, for it never gives up.*

11. When I was a child, I spoke about childish matters, for I saw things like a child and reasoned like a child, but the day came when I matured, and I set aside my childish ways.

12. For now we see but a faint reflection of riddles and mysteries as though reflected in a mirror, but one day we will see face-to-face. My understanding is incomplete now, but one day I will understand everything, just as everything about me has been fully understood.

13. Until then, there are three things that remain: faith, hope, and love - yet love surpasses them all. *So, above all else, let love be the beautiful prize for which you run.*

Once you have embraced Jesus Christ as your Savior and you are walking by His commandments, being led by the Holy Spirit within you, you shall grow quickly. All things will be possible to you because I am a God of deliverance. I operate in the supernatural and all things are possible in

Me. *There is nothing too hard for Me when you walk in faith and obedience unto My Word.*

[I John 4:4 (KJV, paraphrased)]
"You are of Me (God), little children, and have overcome them, [demonic forces] because; greater is He that is within you, than he that is in the world." (The Mighty Holy Spirit within you has overcome the deceiver, Satan)

Revelation 12:11 (TPT)
"They conquered him [the devil] completely through the blood of the Lamb and the powerful Word of His testimony. They triumphed because they did not love and cling to their own lives, even when faced with death."

There still is a spiritual war going on upon Earth today. The only way to win this war is to stand in faith and walk by the Spirit of Truth.

[2 Timothy 1:7 (TPT, paraphrased)]
"For I, God, will never give you the spirit of fear; but the Holy Spirit gives you mighty power, love, and self-control."

Come My children to My table of love. I have reserved a place for you where there is no more sorrow, no more pain. There you will experience My mercy and grace. I move on your behalf to overcome the darkness that pervades the Earth at this hour. I am waiting for you to surrender all to Me. I will bless you beyond all your expectations. Having done all, stand and see the salvation of the Lord.

I love you, Your Father in heaven, God Almighty

JETTA NASTALLY

CHAPTER 20
GOD SPEAKS:

THE PEACE OF GOD

And He arose, and rebuked the wind, and said unto the sea, "Peace, be still". And the wind ceased, and there was a great calm. [**Mark 4:39** (KJV, paraphrased)]

Here is an example of My peace: Jesus was sleeping in the boat when a great storm arose. He was fast asleep untroubled by the storm. His disciples panicked. They were fearful that they would perish in this storm. They awoke Jesus in panic. Jesus arose, rebuking the storm and spoke to the sea, "Peace, be still!" And the wind ceased and there was a great calm. Then *Jesus turned to His disciples and said, "Why are you so fearful? How is it that you have no faith?"* And then they said, "Who can this be, that even the wind and the sea obey Him?"

[**Isaiah 26:3** (NKJV, paraphrased)]
"I will keep him in perfect peace, whose mind is stayed on Me, because he trusts Me, his creator."

I challenge you this day to surrender all to Me and accept My Son as your Savior. Accept the precious gift of salvation that He has provided for you through His sacrificial blood on the Cross at Calvary. You will then receive the gift of *The Holy Spirit who will come dwell within your spirit. He will instruct and guide you in the way you should go. He will guide you with My eyes to see truth and to live in goodness and mercy toward others.*

Psalms 32: 8-11 (KJV)
8. I will instruct thee and teach thee in the way which thou shalt go: I will guide thee with Mine eye.

9. Be ye not as the horse, or as the mule, which have no understanding: whose mouth must be held in with bit and bridle, lest they come near unto thee.
10. Many sorrows shall be to the wicked: but he that trusts in the LORD, mercy shall compass him about.
11. Be glad in the LORD, and rejoice, ye righteous: and shout for joy, all you that are upright in heart.

Yes children, I will always be there for you. Come into My presence through the blood of the Lamb where there is peace, rest, mercy, and love for your soul. *All the trials you have endured have brought you to the place of this total surrender - a place of perfect peace and rest.*

Come dine at My table. I await you. I have waited through the centuries for this hour to embrace My children as My very own family.

I love you with a pure love. Come drink from the well of the water of life where all sorrows drift away and only blessings, peace and love remain.

I love you, Your Father in heaven, God Almighty

CHAPTER 21
GOD SPEAKS:

HAVING THE MIND OF CHRIST
(1 Corinthians 2:16)

What does it mean to have the mind of Christ? If Christ came to visit you, His holiness would overwhelm you because He is pure light. There is no darkness within Him. *To have the mind of Christ means you must walk in holiness.* You live in an impure environment on Earth. *It is impossible to walk in the light of Christ unless you have completely released your vessel to the Lord Jesus Christ - accepting Him as your Lord and Savior and walking in the Spirit of Truth.*

[Philippians 2:5-11 (KJV, paraphrased)]
5. Let this mind be in you, which was also in Christ Jesus,
6. Jesus thought it not robbery to be equal with Me, Father God.
7. But made Himself of no reputation, and took upon Him the form of a servant, and was made in the likeness of men,
8. And being found in fashion as a man, he humbled Himself, and became obedient unto death, even the death of the cross.
9. Wherefore, I, God Almighty, have highly exalted Him, and given Him a name which is above every name,
10. That at the Name of Jesus every knee should bow, of things in heaven, and things in Earth, and things under the Earth,
11. And that every tongue should confess that Jesus Christ is Lord, to the glory of God the Father.

Children, when you surrender all to Me and accept My Son's gift of eternal life, then you have the mind of Christ. Learning to walk in that mind requires your soul to be cleansed of strongholds. Addictions must be broken; they are strongholds of the enemy. They bring forth darkness, depression, and condemnation into your mind.

I Corinthians 2:14-16 (KJV)
14. But *the natural man receives not the things of the Spirit of God: for they are foolishness unto him: neither can he know them, because they are spiritually discerned.*
15. But he that is spiritual judges all things, yet he himself is judged of no man.
16. For who hath known the mind of the Lord, that He may instruct him? But we have the Mind of Christ.

My children be renewed in the Spirit of your mind.

[Ephesians 4:23-32 (TPT, paraphrased)]
23. Now it's time to be made new by every revelation that's been given to you.
24. And to be transformed as you embrace the glorious Christ - within as your new life and live in union with Him! For I have re-created you all over again in His perfect righteousness, and you now belong to Him in the realm of true holiness.
25. So discard every form of dishonesty and lying so that you will be known as one who always speaks the truth, for we all belong to one another.
26. But don't let the passion of your emotions lead you to sin! Don't let anger control you or be fuel for revenge, not for even a day.
27. Don't give the slanderous accuser, the Devil, an opportunity to manipulate you!
28. If any one of you has stolen from someone else, never do it again. Instead, be industrious, earning an honest living, and then you'll have enough to bless those in need.
29. And never let ugly or hateful words come from your mouth, but instead let your words become beautiful gifts

that encourage others; do this by speaking words of grace to help them.

30. The Holy Spirit of God has sealed you in Jesus Christ until you experience your full salvation. So never grieve My spirit or take for granted My holy influence in your life.

31. Lay aside bitter words, temper tantrums, revenge, profanity, and insults.

32. But instead be kind and affectionate toward one another. I have graciously forgiven you, so you must graciously forgive one another in the depths of Christ's love.

***And then renew your mind,* [Romans 12:2** (TPT, paraphrased)]

Stop imitating the ideals and opinions of the culture around you but be inwardly transformed by the Holy Spirit through a total reformation of how you think. This will empower you to discern My will as you live a beautiful life, satisfying and perfect in My eyes.

Prepare Your Hearts and Minds for Action

[I Peter 1:13-16 (TPT, paraphrased)]

13. Prepare your hearts and minds for action! Stay alert and fix your hope firmly on the marvelous grace that is coming to you. For when Jesus Christ is unveiled, a greater measure of grace will be released to you.

14. My obedient children, never again shape your lives by the desires that you followed when you didn't know better.

15. Instead, shape your lives to become like the Holy One who called you.

16. For Scripture says: "You are to be holy, because I am holy."

You must activate and put into practice My word, the holy bible. When you do this, the kingdom of light will flood into your soul. You then become holy as I am holy. You become My beacons of light shining forth my glory into Earth's atmosphere.

Come, draw near to Me and I will draw near to you. Abide in Me and I will abide in you. Make Me your habitation and we will go forth to shine the light of truth to a world that is in gross darkness. I need your vessel to work through. I made it so that My redeemed could speak My will into the Earth and it would come to pass. So come, there are many that need to be delivered and set free.

I love you children, Your Father in heaven, God Almighty

CHAPTER 22
GOD SPEAKS:

YOU ARE A "TREASURE CHEST"
TO CARRY MY GLORY

Notice in My Word the only thing that is forever is the Word of God. All flesh is like grass, it dries up and blows away, but the Word of God remains forever.

Isaiah 40:6-8 (TPT)
6. A voice says, "Cry out!" And I ask, "What should I say?" "All people are as frail as grass, and their elegance is like a wilting wildflower.
7. The grass withers, the flower fades when My breath blows upon it; the people are just like grass!
8. But even though grass withers and the flower fades, My Word stands strong forever!"

[I Peter 1: 4-10 (TPT, paraphrased)]
4. We are reborn into a perfect inheritance that can never perish, never be defiled, and never diminish. It is promised and preserved forever in the heavenly realm for you.
5. Through your faith, My mighty power constantly guards you until your full salvation is ready to be revealed in the last days.
6. May the thought of this cause you to jump for joy, even though lately you've had to put up with the grief of many trials.
7. But these only reveal the sterling core of your faith, which is far more valuable than gold that perishes, for even gold is refined by fire. Your authentic faith will result in even more praise, glory, and honor when Jesus the Anointed One is revealed.
8. You love Christ passionately although you have not seen Him, but through believing in Him you are saturated

with an ecstatic joy, indescribably sublime and immersed in glory.

9. For you are reaping the harvest of your faith - the full salvation promised you - your souls' victory!

10. This salvation was the focus of the prophets who prophesied of this outpouring of grace that was destined for you. They made a careful search and investigation of the meaning of the prophecies I gave them.

My children, having done all things, stand in faith and see My manifest presence of glory come upon you. It shall surely come to pass.

Revelation 3:20 (TPT)

20. Behold, I'm standing at the door, knocking. If your heart is open to hear My voice and you open the door within, I will come in to you and feast with you, and you will feast with Me.

Speak to the mountain and use the Word of God to fight your battles. Jesus did that in the wilderness when Satan came to tempt Him. He just stood on the Word of God; He listened to My Word and He spoke what I instructed Him to speak. Your words when directed by the Holy Spirit have power and authority over the enemy.

Come, you are My treasures on Earth - you are My lights to a dark world. I have placed My glory within you so that you will shine forth in a world enveloped in darkness. Breakthrough comes forth through your vessels when you praise and worship Me in faith while going through your trials. You are the key that unlocks that light to shine forth to the lost who walk in darkness. So, having done all, stand and see the salvation of the Lord.

I wait for you all in great anticipation. *In your resting place in heaven there is no more sorrow, no more pain. Only My goodness and mercy dwell in heaven. My creations on Earth need to see My glory shine from your countenance.* Know that through Christ and through walking in the Spirit of Truth within you, *you will bring forth the harvest.*

Dear children, you are my vessels of glory to shine forth my light into the darkness that surround you.

I love you all so very much!

Your Father in heaven, God Almighty

JETTA NASTALLY

SALVATION CALL:
HOW TO ACCEPT JESUS
INTO YOUR HEART AS YOUR SAVIOR

"But as many as received Him (Jesus Christ), to them gave He power (the right) to become the sons of God, even to them that believe on His name." **John 1:12** (KJV)

Receiving Jesus Christ is an act of your will. Man acts on the Word of God by an act of his will. Man knows he is without a Savior, without an approach to God, without eternal life, so he can look up to God and pray:

PRAYER: Father, I come to You in the Name of the Lord Jesus Christ. I know You will not turn me away, or cast me out, because Your Word says:
"...*him that comes to me I will in no way cast out.*"
John 6:37 (KJV)

PRAYER: I believe in my heart that Jesus Christ is the Son of God. I believe that He died for my sins according to the Scriptures. I believe that He was raised from the dead for my justification, according to the Scriptures. 'Justification' means that I might be set right with God. I believe that because of His death, burial, and resurrection, I am set right with God. So, I receive Jesus as My Savior, and I confess Him as My Lord. Your Word says:
"*Whosoever shall call upon the name of the Lord shall be saved.*" *Romans 10:13 (KJV)*

PRAYER: I am calling on Your name now, so I know I am saved, And Your Word says:
"*If you shall confess with your mouth the Lord Jesus and shall believe in your heart that God has raised*

Him from the dead, you shall be saved." **Romans 10:9** (KJV)

PRAYER: I confess with my mouth and I believe in my heart what the Word of God says. So, I know I am saved. Your Word says:
"...with the heart, man believes unto righteousness." **2 Corinthians 5:21** (KJV)

PRAYER: And with my heart I believe that I am made right with God for Your Word says:
"...with the mouth, confession is made unto salvation" **Romans 10:10** (KJV)

PRAYER: *So, with my mouth I confess that I am saved. Thank You Lord for this great miracle of salvation that you have given me this day![1]*

END NOTES:

SALVATION CALL:
1. Hagin, Kenneth E. (Sr.), *In Him*, Rhema Bible Church, aka, Kenneth Hagin Ministries, Inc., 1988

ABOUT THE AUTHOR

TESTIMONY OF JETTA NASTALLY

This book comes forth because I have had a near death experience in my life that brought me to my knees and caused me to surrender all to God. It has allowed me to surrender my life completely to the Lord Jesus Christ. I now walk by the Spirit of Life within me (the Holy Spirit) and have overcome the spirit of death. I was scammed out of all my retirement monies and this is my personal story of the miraculous recovery that God performed on my behalf. God has asked me to share my experience with others so they too can be set free.

For the past two years, God has hidden me away to teach me the language of the Holy Spirit. I've learned to be sensitive to His voice and activate on Earth what He instructs me to speak forth. I speak God's Word and it brings forth the blessings of God. Everything that Satan stole from me will come back to me in excess. When the fullness of this transpires, I will be able to further the Kingdom of God financially. It is my desire that none should perish, but all should come to the truth of the Word of God. Only through the light of God's Word will the veil of deception be removed from the blind eyes and deaf ears of the lost. Only through intercession, worship, and bringing forth the Glory of God into the atmosphere shall this come to pass. The cry of my heart is to see all receive the gift of salvation through Jesus Christ. No one should have to spend eternity in hell - a very real kingdom of torment and gross darkness.

This is a story of how I learned to surrender all to God and walk in the Spirit of Truth overcoming the evil spirits of darkness.

SHORT BIOGRAPHY OF JETTA NASTALLY

I am currently an ordained minister of the gospel of the Lord Jesus Christ under the ministry of Joan Hunter Ministries. The church I attend is Eastgate Ministries where Pastor Carolyn Sissom teaches the pure Word of God - teaching us how to use the weapons of the Word to fight spiritual warfare against the devil.

I graduated from two universities. I received my bachelor's degree in business at Woodbury University in Los Angeles, California; I received my master's degree through National University in San Diego, California.

Ever since I have been saved, I have known that God wanted to write a book through my vessel. I knew this book had to be written by Him. After 47 years of waiting, this book comes forth. The contents of God's book through me give the hopeless encouragement to believe they have purpose and destiny. This book teaches all how to overcome the evil ploys of the devil.

I trust that the anointing on this book will part your Red Sea, and you will cross over to your promise land. God loves you so. He sent His Son to die on the Cross of Calvary to set you free. He came to give you life more abundantly, filled with righteousness, peace, and joy in the Holy Spirit. You need only to reach out and take His hand. He is waiting to set you free.

Ministry Contact Information:

Ask, Seek and Knock Ministries
PO Box 5254
Katy, TX 77491

www.ingramcontent.com/pod-product-compliance
Lightning Source LLC
Chambersburg PA
CBHW052003090426
42741CB00008B/1529